A HISTORY OF
DRAGONS

A HISTORY OF DRAGONS

THEIR INFLUENCE ON LIFE AND CULTURE

SARAH-BETH WATKINS

PEN & SWORD
HISTORY

AN IMPRINT OF PEN & SWORD BOOKS LTD.
YORKSHIRE – PHILADELPHIA

First published in Great Britain in 2024 by
PEN AND SWORD HISTORY
An imprint of
Pen & Sword Books Ltd
Yorkshire – Philadelphia

ISBN 978 1 39905 883 4

Typeset in Times New Roman 12/16 by
SJmagic DESIGN SERVICES, India.
Printed and bound in the UK by CPI Group (UK) Ltd.

Pen & Sword Books Limited incorporates the imprints of Atlas, Archaeology,
Aviation, Discovery, Family History, Fiction, History, Maritime, Military,
Military Classics, Politics, Select, Transport, True Crime, Air World, Frontline
Publishing, Leo Cooper, Remember When, Seaforth Publishing, The Praetorian
Press, Wharncliffe Local History, Wharncliffe Transport, Wharncliffe True Crime
and White Owl.

For a complete list of Pen & Sword titles please contact
PEN & SWORD BOOKS LIMITED
George House, Units 12 & 13, Beevor Street, Off Pontefract Road,
Barnsley, South Yorkshire, S71 1HN, England
E-mail: enquiries@pen-and-sword.co.uk
Website: www.pen-and-sword.co.uk

or

PEN AND SWORD BOOKS
1950 Lawrence Rd, Havertown, PA 19083, USA
E-mail: uspen-and-sword@casematepublishers.com
Website: www.penandswordbooks.com

FSC
www.fsc.org
MIX
Paper | Supporting
responsible forestry
FSC® C013604

Contents

Introduction

This book takes a comprehensive look at dragons, our most popular and beloved mythological creature, from both a cultural and historical perspective. From Chinese Imperial dragons to the worms and wyverns of English folklore, dragons appear in myths and legends around the world and throughout history. The first part of this book charts the evolution of the dragon from their origins, through early myths and folklore, as a creature of Satan and on to a cuddly Toothless and all that's in between. In the second part, we will look at dragon tales from the West and East to reveal how our love of dragons is recorded in many different stories.

We begin by looking at the origins of dragons and some of the theories put forward as to why they are such a part of our psyche. We may think we know what a dragon looks like, but across cultures their depictions differ and we look at some of these variations in chapter two. Chapter three takes a look at the early myths and chapter four takes us to Greece, Rome and early civilisations to see how the dragon appeared there. The Vikings had a different take on this magical and majestical beast as we will see in chapter five and chapter six shows us a change in beliefs around the dragon and how it began to be used as a metaphor to signify dark forces. Chapter seven takes a closer look at the medieval dragon and the tales in which it appeared. Throughout, we will encounter many old tales of dragons that show us just how their imagery was used and how they influenced life and culture but chapters eight and nine, especially, feature some of the best stories of dragons from both western and eastern cultures. The final chapter looks at how dragons have been portrayed in film and fiction up to the present day.

Chapter 1

Origins of the World Dragon

How can such a fantastical creature be a global phenomenon and appear in mythologies, legends and cultures across the world? From our very first recorded and depicted myths, dragons have appeared, meaning different things to different people admittedly, but appear they have, nonetheless. Comparative mythology is a field of study that looks at myths from different cultures to identify shared themes and motifs. Things like creation stories, the world tree, founding myths, gods and goddesses and you guessed it — the dragon — appear time and time again. It may be in different guises, in different tales, as benevolent or chaotic but the dragon has a cultural history that spans time and continents.

What is most intriguing is that the concept of the dragon — in whatever form it took (and there are many of them as we shall see!) — is one of our oldest legends and exists simultaneously in cultures that were not in touch with each other in the age before travel. In such isolated places their origins cannot be put down to transmission; stories that were shared between cultures. The dragon, then, could be said to be a part of the collective unconscious, a term created by the influential psychiatrist, Carl Jung, who believed there was a form of the unconscious that was common to all mankind as a whole and shared amongst societies.

Tales of dragons predate organised religion and although their stories were later Christianised and the dragon demonised, in many early tales and creation myths the dragon is something else: a snakelike creature that circled the world; a sea monster that held back the tides; a spiny dragon who escaped the Great Flood; a dragon whose body made up the earth and the sky. They were there from the very beginning when man was making sense of the world and they played a part in the formation of our universe. Many of these early depictions are of creatures that lived in water — sea serpents and lake wyrms — and are not what we would typically think of as a dragon. But from these roots our winged, fire-breathing, jewel-guarding dragons were born.

But dragons don't only appear in myth. There was real belief in these creatures and written records that testify to their existence. Pliny the Elder, a Roman naturalist and philosopher, discusses dragons in his *Naturalis Historia* or Natural History, first published in 1469. What he deemed to be dragons are featured in a chapter that also includes crocodiles, snakes and other reptiles, which speaks to their watery origins. He could, of course, have been referring to the biggest of snakes but his descriptions are intriguing. In Book Eight of *Natural History*, he writes:

> Elephants breed in that part of Affricke which lyeth beyond the deserts ... India bringeth forth the biggest: as also the dragons that are continually at variance with them, and evermore fighting, and those of such greatnesse, that they can easily claspe and wind round about the Elephants, and withall tye them fast with a knot.

He also mentions:

> ... the dragons ware hereof, entangle and snarle his feet and legges first with their taile: the Elephants on the other side, undoe those knots wiht their trunke as with a hand ... the principall thing the dragons make at, is the eye ... Now these dragons are so big withall, that they be able to receive all the Elephants bloud. Thus they are sucked drie, untill they fall down dead.

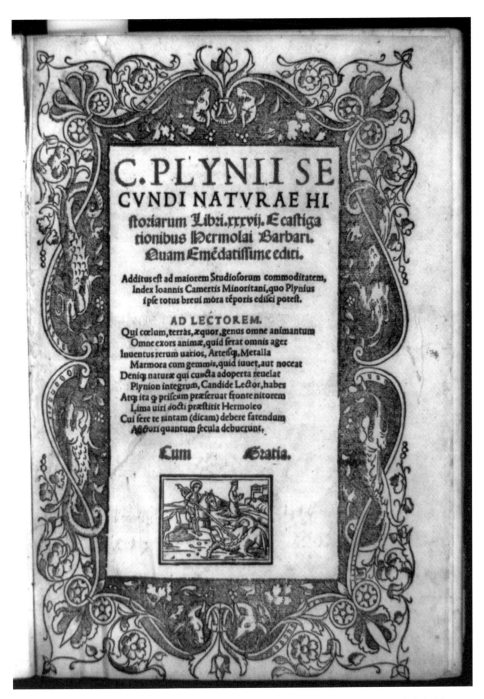

Title page of Pliny's *Naturalis Historia*, with a decorative border of dolphins and illustration of St Michael lancing a dragon.

And that these dragons reached 30 feet long:

> ... there be serpents among the Indians grown to that bignesse, that they are able to swallow stags or buls all whole ... Attilius Regulus, generall under the Romanes, during the warres against the Carthaginians, assailed a Serpent neere the river Bagrada, which caried in length 120 foot.

Pliny the Elder wasn't exaggerating and there are several accounts of a serpent or dragon that attacked the Roman army and whose body was sent back to Rome. So there are historical accounts of dragons and they are as wide and varied as the different types of dragons themselves. The *Anglo-Saxon Chronicle* entry for AD 793 states:

> This year came dreadful fore-warnings over the land of the Northumbrians, terrifying the people most woefully: these were immense sheets of light rushing through the air, and whirlwinds, and fiery dragons flying across the firmament.

The *Annals of Ulster* entry from AD 735 states, 'A huge dragon was seen, with great thunder after it, at the end of autumn' and in AD 746 it records, 'Dragons were seen in the sky'. These sightings can maybe be explained by weather phenomena, such as comets or meteors, but the fact that these dragons were personified as creatures and depicted as such in works like medieval bestiaries and natural history books both speaks to something more and adds to more confusion about what a dragon really was.

Some authors have posited that dragons were actual beasts like Archosaurs (large reptiles with no wings) or Pterosaurs (reptiles with wings that flew in the skies when dinosaurs walked the earth). As recently as 2022, scientists in Argentina discovered a new species of flying reptile, Thanatosdrakon Amaru (the dragon of death), with a

A dragon from *Medieval Bestiary*, Harley MS 3244.

30 feet wing span, a long neck and large head, and a beak that lived during the Late Cretaceous period about 86 million years ago.

Chang Qu, a Chinese historian from the 4th century BC, who wrote the *Chronicles of Huayang* or *Records of the States South of Mount Hua*, the oldest extant regional history of China, described the finding of dragon bones at Wucheng, in what is now Sichuan Province (south-western China). In 1676, Reverend Robert Plot, a curator of an English museum, found a large thigh bone and attributed it to a race of giants. It wasn't until 1841/1842, that Richard Owen came to the conclusion, after examining fossil finds, that there were ever dinosaurs. So humans had been finding bones for centuries not knowing what they were and perhaps there have been dragon bones that have long since perished — nobody can say for sure.

Dissenters will say, 'but there are no bones, and no actual evidence of dragons', but the scientists who found Thanatosdrakon Amaru state that because the bones are fine and thin, skeletons rarely survive. The fantasy writer, Richard Carpenter, in a 1993 interview came to the conclusion that dragons had hollow bones so they could fly, so if the evidence is not there it doesn't necessarily mean they did not exist, just that their bones did not survive. Whether or not dragons were ever real creatures is an argument that could run and run. What

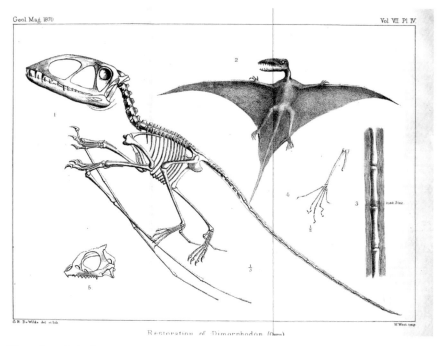

Geol Mag 1870

Vol VII Pl IV

G R De Wilde del et lith

W West imp

Restoration of Dimorphodon (Owen)

Pterodactyl skeleton.

matters more is that the idea of them started with creation myths and never went away. Dragons evolved from a belief in their existence to becoming firmly enshrined in our imagination.

Nature certainly gives us clues as to what a dragon might have looked like if it truly did walk the earth. Komodo dragons, bearded dragons, crocodiles, even water creatures like the alligator gar or sea dragons all show us how fantastical nature can be and it's not a far stretch of the imagination to see how easily dragons could have existed.

Because the earliest attested dragons all resemble snakes or have snake-like attributes, it has been suggested that dragons are the creation of our innate fear of serpents. In early mythology dragons and serpents are very similar and appear interchangeable, but as time progressed they separated more fully and the dragon took on its own mythology. Snakes were revered for what appeared to be their conquest of death. Because they shed their skin, they were believed to die but be reborn, thus having magical powers of transformation. Primates fear snakes and another theory is that during our evolution we have retained this fear of snakes, as well as eagles and lions, which combine to make for a dragon-like creature.

In Carl Sagan's book *The Dragons of Eden* he asks the question whether the subconscious fear we have of monsters today is the result of evolutionary responses stemming from primates' fear of dragons and owls. He cites Charles Darwin who questioned whether the very real fears children have of monsters under the bed are inherited effects of real dangers and abject superstitions from ancient 'savage' times. Are they then, a warning in our psyche from early evolution alerting us to a danger that is no longer real? But Sagan also posits: 'Is it possible that dragons posed a problem for our protohuman ancestors of a few million years ago, and that the terror they evoked and the deaths they caused helped bring about the evolution of human intelligence?'

Illustration of a winged, fire-breathing dragon by Friedrich Justin Bertuch from 1806.

Whether they actually existed or whether the fear developed by primates and early man has evolved into our fear of monsters today, points to there being more to the concept of the dragon than just as a mythical figure.

Do we have psychological reasons to fear dragons? In MacLean's Triune Brain model, the basal ganglia, parts of the brain responsible primarily for motor control, are referred to as the reptilian or primal brain. This reptile brain controls our automatic self-preserving behaviour patterns, which ensure our survival with things like our fight or flight response. If a dragon scares us, we run from it or fight it which is a motif we will see repeating in early literature and dragon slaying tales. Having demonised the dragon over time in the Western world, it has become an archetype for fear, anxiety and obstacles within us that need banishing. In some psychological circles, it has become a metaphor for slaying the dragon within and vanquishing our demons, in order to find gold — the truth within ourselves. Sagan questioned whether when we fear dragons, we are actually fearing those parts of ourselves that we are uncomfortable with, or that we feel unhappy about and that from a psychological perspective, we need to address.

J.J. Cohen in his book *Monster Culture* expands on monster theory with seven theses to explain why we are so intrigued by creatures such as dragons and other fantastical creatures. The first thesis is that 'the monster's body is a cultural body'; in essence a creature is born out of a culture's need. So if we consider how dragons have been part of origin myths, it goes some way to explaining why they were created: for humans to make sense of the world and in some respects to mirror societies' fears. Cohen says that the 'monster inhabits the gap between the time of upheaval that created it and the moment which it is received to be born again'. In other words it is conceived and given meaning by a culture, but as cultures and societies change through time it will also be re-interpreted in a new historical, social, and cultural context. If we look at the evolution of the dragon from a monster to be feared to a cuddly pet to be adored, we can see that our psychological need for dragons has changed. From the evil and Satanic creature of

THE BEAUTIFUL WOMAN SOOTHES THE SERPENT-KING

Taken from *The Violet Fairy Book* (1906).

Christianity to the friendly Zog or Toothless, dragons are otherworldly and by being such they call to us on a subconscious level.

So we could ask why they are now seen as cute and cuddly? Dragons are no longer feared perhaps because they no longer need to be. We may want them to be real, look for evidence that they did indeed exist and wish to see them in the skies once more but we know it's not going to happen. Dragons will remain in the myths and stories of cultures and they no longer pose a threat. Nowadays, literature, art, TV and film depict friendlier versions than the fire-breathing, maiden-eating dragons of yore. From Dreamwork's Toothless (*How to Train Your Dragon*) to Julia Donaldson's Zog or the endearing 'Puff the Magic Dragon' song by Peter, Paul and Mary that tells of what happens when a dragon is no longer loved, children are now raised seeing and hearing of friendly dragons. Dragons that are likeable, magical and mystical creatures. Dragons that are no longer monsters under the bed. So instead of dying out from our collective unconscious, they have remained, transformed throughout history, and have become one of our favourite fantastical creatures. What's more they are not going anywhere; dragons are here to stay.

Chapter 2

Types of Dragons

In the Western world we think of a dragon as having four limbs, huge wings, breathing fire and guarding treasure. But across the globe and throughout myth and time, what constitutes a dragon varies. What pictures come to mind when you think of a dragon? Is it a destructive creature as depicted in the books and series *Game of Thrones*, a more gentle creature as in the film *Dragonheart* or a cartoon-like image like Toothless in *How to Train your Dragon*?

Types of dragons vary across the continents of Asia, Africa, North America, South America, Europe, and Australia. The only continent

The Welsh flag.

to not have dragon stories is Antarctica because it has never had an indigenous population. Where there be humans, there also be dragons!

The Western dragon or European dragon is often depicted as mentioned above with four legs and two large wings. He breathes fire, is covered with reptilian scales and has an immense tail. Think

St George and the dragon.

of the dragon that fought with St George or the Welsh dragon, Y Ddraig Goch, meaning 'the red dragon', that appears on the national flag of Wales.

Henry VII had a similar dragon too on his standard as he rode into battle to denote his Welsh heritage and this was carried into St Paul's Cathedral after his victory at Bosworth. Dragons have been adopted by royalty and nobility on their crests and standards but stories of them stayed alive in common belief for centuries.

If we are looking for stories of typical dragons we can look no further than British folklore which is rife with tales of magnificent beasts, often paired with heroes and maidens or depicted as fire-breathing treasure hoarders. *The Dragon of Wantley* is a British legend from South Yorkshire, originally told in a ballad of 1685:

> This dragon had two furious wings,
> Each one upon each shoulder;
> With a sting in his tail as long as a flail
> Which made him bolder and bolder.
> He had long claws, and in his jaws
> Four and forty teeth of iron;
> With a hide as tough as any buff,
> Which did him round environ.

Wantley or Wharncliffe was home to this dragon who met his end in an unusual way. The villagers of Wantley approached a knight, Moore of Moore Hall, to help them rid the town of this beast who ate cattle, trees, houses and churches — quite the appetite! Moore kitted himself out in a suite of Sheffield armour covered in spikes and lay in wait for the creature that was causing so much havoc. There are different endings of this tale, some cleaner than others! One version has the dragon being struck in the neck, others like this one are a little coarser:

> As he came like a lout, so he turned him about,
> And hit him a kick on the arse.

The Dragon of Wantley.

'Oh,' quoth the Dragon, with a deep sigh,
And turned six times together.
Sobbing and tearing, cursing and swearing,
Out of his throat of leather:
'Moore of Moore Hall! O thou rascal!
Would I had seen thee never!
With the thing at thy foot thou hast pricked my arse-gut,
And I'm quite undone forever.'

But we don't only have tales of two-winged, four legged dragons. The wyvern by contrast has only two legs and two wings and is often thought of as a smaller and weaker type of dragon. It is a cross between a Western dragon and a worm (or wyrm) as discussed below. The name comes from the Latin *vīpera* meaning snake. Often used in medieval heraldry, one example is the personal crest of Thomas Crouchback (1278–1322), an earl of Lancaster and Leicester. A wyvern was also incorporated into the Arms of the City of Leicester. A white wyvern with red and white wounds showing sits atop the city's crest.

So not only are our books, films and TV flooded with descriptions and depictions of what constitutes a dragon, they have a long historical basis both in primary sources as real creatures and as more fantastical creatures in myth and folklore. These tales and legends can have different iterations, different endings, different protagonists, and different types of dragons depending on what part of the world they come from. There really is a dragon tale for everyone!

Maud and the Mordiford Wyvern is another example of a legend that has various different endings. Set in the Herefordshire village of Mordiford, a young girl called Maud was walking in the woods when she found a bright green, baby wyvern. She took him home to keep as a pet but her parents, fearing what he would become, told her to take it back from whence it came.

Maud sort of did as she was told but she took him to her hiding place amongst the trees and visited him daily, bringing him milk and watching as her baby wyvern grew into an adult. Milk would not sustain him after a time and so the wyvern began to eat chickens, sheep, and cows. And when the local farmers tried to stop him, he ate them too! The only person he would not harm was Maud.

The way the wyvern met his end varies from being shot, stabbed or twisted around a spiked barrel with the hero dying from the wyvern's poisonous last breath. But another ending references a local family, the Garstons, sending out one of their men to find the dragon. When he does, he throws a lance at the wyvern's neck and Maud, distraught, cradles her pet as he dies.

Wyrms (lindworms or worms) are dragons without legs with worm-like bodies and survive in some of the oldest legends. Associated with water, they have been described as slithering out of a well, bog or lake to attack an unsuspecting passer-by. Usually found in European tales, some of the most well-known include the tales of the *Lambton Worm*, the *Laidly Worm of Spindleston Heugh*, the *Worm of Sockburn*, the *Mester Stoor Worm* and the *Worm of Linton*.

The Sockburn worm (also described as a wyvern) was ravaging the local countryside and Sir John Conyers, a member of a wealthy local family, agreed to do away with the beast. He attacked the worm with his falchion (a sword with a slightly curved blade), and after accomplishing his task was given lands around the village as his reward. This tale may have inspired Lewis Carroll to write his well-known poem about the Jabberwocky — 'Beware the Jabberwock, my son! The jaws that bite, the claws that catch!'

A wyvern crest.

To this day Conyer's falchion still hangs in Durham Cathedral and whenever a new Bishop of Durham enters the Diocese for the first time a welcoming ceremony is conducted on the bridge that crosses the River Tee, with the words:

> My Lord Bishop, I hereby present you with the falchion wherewith the champion Conyers slew the worm, dragon or fiery serpent which destroyed man, woman and child; in memory of which the king then reigning gave him the manor of Sockburn, to hold by this tenure, that upon first entrance of every bishop into the county the falchion should be presented.

The lindworm or lindorm from Sweden by comparison lives in the forest in caves or between large rocks. It is snakelike with no limbs or wings but instead has dorsal type fins along its back. In the nineteenth century Swedish folklorist, Gunnar Olof Hyltén-Cavallius, tried to prove dragons were real and collected around fifty eyewitness reports. In 1884 he offered a reward for a captured specimen, dead or alive, but he was mocked by Swedish scholars as no such specimen was ever found. Still the lindworm stayed alive in folktales such as the *Lindworm Prince*. In this tale a queen gives birth to twins. On the advice of an old crone she eats two onions before their birth, the first unpeeled resulting in her first child being a lindworm and the second being human. When the youngest son wants to find a bride, the lindworm insists that a bride be found for him too. But unhappy with them all he decides to eat them until a young girl approaches him dressed in many layers of clothes. He tells her to take off her clothes but she insists for every layer she takes off, he must shed a skin. As she takes off her final layer, he sheds his final skin and revealed underneath is the prince he was really meant to be.

Whilst we mainly associate dragons with breathing fire, many of the tales and legends surrounding them are of water. As we've seen

A depiction of a worm or lindworm.

with wyrms or worms, they live in wet, damp places. From early legends of monstrous beasts like the Greek Hydra, Biblical Leviathan and Norse Jörmungandr to the Knuckers of Sussex, these creatures are far more serpent-like.

Knucker, from the Old English word nicor, meaning 'water dragon', live in knuckerholes or ponds throughout Sussex and are serpent-like with small wings and a deadly, hissing mouth. Stories like the *Lyminster Knucker* have changed and been adapted over the years. As with *St George and the Dragon*, sometimes it's a saint or knight that does away with the beast but as in one version of the *Lyminster Knucker*, it can be an ordinary, but clever, man. The tale begins:

They do say, that a dunnamany years ago there was a gert dragon lived in that big pond there, Knucker his name was, and Knucker Hole we calls it to-day. And thisyer ole dragon, you know, he uster goo spannelling about the Brooks by night to see what he could pick up for supper, like few horses, or cows maybe, he'd snap 'em up soon as look at 'em. Then bimeby he took to sitting top o' Causeway, and anybody come along there, he'd lick 'em up, like a toad licking flies off a stone.

But young Jim Puttock had a plan and he asked the local smith for a big iron pot, the miller for flour and the local woodmen to build a big fire. On it he placed the pot and made 'the biggest pudden' that was ever seen'. Then he went to find the knucker.

'How do, Man.'

'How do, Dragon?' says Jim.

'What you got there?' says Dragon, sniffing.

'Pudden,' says Jim.

'Pudden?' says Knucker. 'What be that?'

'Just you try,' says Jim.

So Jim fed him the pudding and the knucker said he wouldn't mind some more so Jim told him he'd be back that afternoon. But the pudding didn't go down too well as before long the people of

Lyminster could hear the knucker roaring and bellowing. On his return the knucker said to Jim:

'Don't you dare bring me no more o' that 'ere pudden, young marn!'

'Why?' says Jim. 'What's matter?'

'Colly wobbles,' says the Dragon. 'Do set so heavy on me I can't stand un, nohows in de wurreld.'

'Shudn't bolt it so,' says Jim, 'but never mind, I got a pill here, soon cure that.'

'Where?' says Knucker.

'Here,' says Jim.

And unfortunately for the knucker, Jim's cure was to cut off his head with an axe!

Ireland too has its fair share of watery dragon stories. In October 1871, a newspaper in County Clare reported:

A party of strangers staying at Kilkee, composed of several ladies and some gentlemen, one of whom is a well-known clergyman in the north of Ireland, were out for a walk at a place known as the Diamond Rocks. All of a sudden, their attention was arrested by the appearance of an extraordinary monster, who rose from the surface of the water about seventy yards from the place where they were standing. It had an enormous head, shaped somewhat like a horse, while behind the head and on the neck was a huge mane of seaweed-looking water; the eyes were large and glaring, and, by the appearance of the water behind, a vast body seemed to be beneath the waves.

But there are also other Irish legends including that of two types of mythological dragon that appear in Cath Maige Mucrama, or The Battle of Mag Mucrama, found in *The Book of Leinster,* a medieval Irish manuscript, compiled c.1160:

Now Mag Mucrima [was so called from] magic pigs that had come out of the cave of Crúachain. That is Ireland's gate to Hell. Out of it too came the swarm of three-headed creatures that laid Ireland waste until Amairgene father of Conall Cernach, fighting alone, destroyed it in the presence of all the Ulaid.

Out of it also had come the saffron-coloured bird-flock and they withered up everything in Ireland that their breath touched until the Ulaid killed them with their slings.

So we have a swarm of three-headed creatures and a swarm of fire-breathing birds that came out of the gate to hell. The three-headed dragon continues its story in the Irish folktales of *Ellén Trechend*.

France has a particularly rich history of dragons from vouivres, guivres, gargouilles, tarasques and the peluda. The peluda or 'shaggy beast' was a serpent-like dragon covered in poison-tipped spines that lived in the River Huisne after being denied a place on Noah's Ark. It could cause floods and shoot fire from its mouth, destroying crops, livestock and humans and could also whip its tail in a frenzy to create havoc. But one day it captured l'Agnelle (Little Lamb), a virtuous maiden who was championed by her fiancé who killed the peluda with a well-aimed blow to its tail — its most vulnerable spot.

The vouivre is always female and is a winged dragon but instead of eyes, she has a single large ruby or diamond in her head that helps guide her as she flies. When she bathes, the jewel is removed leaving her blind and vulnerable to attack. She has been depicted in many ways including being half-human but is nearly always associated with precious jewels. The vouivre of La Baume is covered in pearls and other gems which sometimes drops as she takes to the air, whilst in Boëge, she wears a golden necklace.

In the Basque region, west of the Pyrenees, there is a dragon with seven heads. The 'herensuge' is serpent-like with no wings. He is a cave-dweller associated with the god Sugaar. A source mentions

The peluda on the cover of a French pamphlet (1889).

that as the heads grow to maturity they fall off the dragon to create baby herensuge! One story tells of a young man who came across an elderly woman whilst walking one day. She asked him for just a piece of the delicious-looking cake he was carrying. Being a good sort, he offered her the whole cake instead and to reward him for his kindness she gave him the gift of a stick that could kill with a single blow.

The young man looked for work at a local palace and was given the job of shepherd, guarding the royal flock of sheep. His powerful stick became extremely useful for despatching creatures that preyed on the sheep but one day, in a bargain to save its life, one of the predators told the young man of another palace, hidden in the woods, where he would find great riches.

The hero in this tale sets off to find this wonderful palace but when he finds it, people tell him of the herensuge that they are afraid of. The people there must draw lots to see who will be given as a sacrifice to appease the hungry dragon. The palace is in uproar as it is now the princess' turn to be sacrificed. The young man cannot let that happen and so when it is time for the princess to meet her fate, he goes with her into the mountains. As the herensuge approaches, the young man lunges forth with his trusty stick and kills each head in turn. Once the creature has been defeated, he receives his ultimate reward — the hand of the princess in marriage — a common theme in many dragon tales.

In Cyprus, pyrausta dragons appear as a tiny insect-like dragons. Pyraustas have wings like butterflies or moths, four limbs, and large shining black eyes. They are born of fire and must never stray too far from the flames, living in the furnaces of Cyprus. As Pliny the Elder described them:

> That element, also, which is so destructive to matter, produces certain animals; for in the copper-smelting furnaces of Cyprus, in the very midst of the fire, there is to be seen flying about a four-footed animal with wings,

the size of a large fly: this creature is called the "pyrallis," and by some the "pyrausta." So long as it remains in the fire it will live, but if it comes out and flies a little distance from it, it will instantly die.

From early times then, Western dragons appear in myths and legends as dragons, wyverns, wyrms or knuckers and much much more. But tales and legends of dragons appear in many diverse cultures and they can be strikingly different.

For instance, the Eastern dragon has a different appearance; a more serpentine body with four legs and no wings. Imperial dragons have five toes, Chinese dragons four and Japanese three. Unlike Western dragons who are notorious for eating people and wreaking havoc, thus needing a hero to vanquish them, Eastern dragons don't breathe fire and are auspicious; they are weather lords, the protectors of heaven and Imperial emperors and they symbolise power, good luck and strength. They have also remained stable as a type throughout Eastern history whereas the Western dragon has changed into many different forms.

ETC Werner wrote in his *Dictionary of Chinese Mythology* of a real dragon encounter in 1931:

The following incident, which occurred in May 1931, indicates the persistence of beliefs [in dragons]. A scaled and horned dragon, believed by many to be a supernatural creature, has made its appearance in Kiangsi … Mr Huang writes from Nanchang that the dragon was seen on the Kan River, the principal river in Kiangsi, about half a month ago … as the Book of History recorded that 2,000 years ago the people used to offer the fairest maiden every year to the Ho Po, or God of the River, to be his concubine, it is now suggested that some suitable sacrifice should be presented to the dragon. It is said that if his wrath is appeased, the flood will subside. On the

A Japanese dragon, colour engraving on wood. Chinese school, 19th century.

other hand, if nothing is done to please the creature, it would make the Kiangsi people suffer more besides the Flood …

The Han dynasty scholar Wang Fu recorded the appearance of a Chinese dragon:

> The people paint the dragon's shape with a horse's head and a snake's tail. Further, there are expressions as 'three joints' and 'nine resemblances' (of the dragon), to wit: from head to shoulder, from shoulder to breast, from breast to tail. These are the joints; as to the nine resemblances, they are the following: his antlers resemble those of a stag, his head that of a camel, his eyes those of a demon, his neck that of a snake, his belly that of a clam, his scales those of a carp, his claws those of an eagle, his soles those of a tiger, his ears those of a cow. Upon his head he has a thing like a broad eminence (a big lump), called [chimu]. If a dragon has no [chimu], he cannot ascend to the sky.

And L Joly in his book *Legend in Japanese Art*, gives us more details of how an Eastern dragon looks:

> The Chinese call the Dragon Lung because it is deaf; it is the largest of scaly animals, and it has nine characteristics. Its head is like a camel's, its horns like a deer's, its eyes like a hare's (a devil's?), its ears like a bull's, its neck like a iguana's, its scales like those of a carp its paws like a tiger's, and its claws like an eagle's. It has nine times nine scales, it being the extreme or lucky number.
>
> On each side of its mouth are whiskers, under its chin a bright pearl, on the top of its head the POH SHAN or foot rule, without which it cannot ascend to Heaven.

The scales of its throat are reversed. Its breath changes into clouds, from which come either fire or rain. The dragon is fond of the flesh of sparrows and swallows, it dreads the centipede and silk dyed of five colours. It is also afraid of iron. In front of its horns it carries a pearl of bluish colour, striated with more or less symbolical lines. It has the power of invisibility and of transformation at will, it is able to shrink or to increase in size without limits.

As Joly mentions, Eastern dragons are often depicted with a pearl under their chin symbolising wisdom, power and spiritual energy. But there are many different interpretations of the pearl and it has also been seen to represent the moon, thunder, the sun, or life. Here is one such tale:

Long ago, there lived in China a young boy called Chi Yu. Chi Yu and his mother lived in a humble cottage close to rolling lush green meadows. Every morning Chi Yu would go to cut this fertile grass and sell it to the farmer to feed his cows but one year the grass did not grow. There was no rain and the meadow turned to dust. Chi Yu searched further and further afield to find green grass for the farmer until one day he travelled as far as the tall hills and there he found one patch of the lushest grass he had ever seen. He gathered it all up in his basket and took it to the farmer and every day he trekked back to the tall hills and cut it again and again.

Then one day as he cut the grass with his sickle he saw something shiny and small — a lovely golden pearl. He took it home and placed it in a jar half-full of rice for safekeeping. The next day he saw that the jar was brimming with rice. He emptied it and once more it filled again. There was something wonderous and magical about that golden pearl!

When the farmer heard of this, he wanted the pearl for himself. Chin Yu refused to sell it to him, no matter how much he pleaded,

A fisherboy dived into the water and brought up a pearl from beneath the chin of a black dragon. From *The Chinese Fairy Book*.

so in the dark of night the farmer crept into Chin Yu's house that he shared with his mother and tried to steal it but Chin Yu woke up and seeing what the farmer was about, ran to the jar and grabbing the pearl, swallowed it down.

But as he swallowed it, it burnt. It burnt his tongue, his throat, his stomach. He felt hot and to quench his thirst he drank all the water in the house, then ran outside to drink from a pond, a stream, a lake — whatever he could find. He drank all the water in the nearby village and still it wasn't enough. And then he began to breathe fire. And as he breathed fire, Chin Yu changed into a magnificent dragon, resplendent in all his glory and so he took to the skies and flew far, far away across those tall hills and beyond.

The pearl in this story then bestows dragonhood and Chin Yu changes into a magnificent beast.

Japanese dragons are mostly water-based and associated with the sea, rivers or rain. Tales of humans that turn into dragons like Chin Yu are less common but there is the tale of Kiyohime from around the eleventh century:

Kiyohime lived with her father Masago no Shōji and every year they were visited by a young priest named Anchin, on a pilgrimage from Mutsu to the Kumano shrine, who rested at their manor. Kiyohime looked forward to Anchin's visits and over the years fell

Section of the scroll *Dōjōji Engi Emaki*, illustrating the story where the serpent burns the bell, killing the monk.

in love with him. Jokingly he told the young girl that he would marry her when she grew up so when Kiyohime reached marriageable age, she reminded him of his promise. Anchin had never truly intended to marry her and the next time he was due to visit, he avoided the manor and carried on to the Dojo-ji temple, hailing a boatman to take him across the Hidaka river.

So upset was Kiyohime that she dove straight into the turbulent river and as her body was bruised and battered by the waves, she turned into a water dragon which enabled her to cross the raging river and chase Anchin to the Dojo-ji temple.

Seeing her now monstrous form, Anchin asked the priests of Dojo-ji for help and they hid him under the bronze temple bell. But Kiyohime could smell him and so she coiled herself around it. She banged the bell with her tail and then heated it with her flaming breath until Anchin was roasted inside. This is one tale where the dragon is a vessel for revenge although Kiyohime also died, as after she killed Anchin she threw herself back into the Hidaka river to drown.

In North and South America, a mixture of sea serpents, lizards, fingered or winged deities and chimaeras all have dragon-like aspects. The horned serpent is particularly common in Native American mythology. To the Cherokee it was known as Uktena. James Mooney,

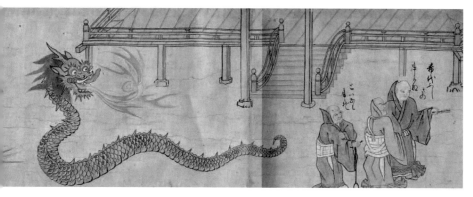

Kiyohime and the priests of Dojo-ji.

an ethnographer, lived for many years with Cherokee tribes and described it as:

> Those who know say the Uktena is a great snake, as large around as a tree trunk, with horns on its head, and a bright blazing crest like a diamond on its forehead, and scales glowing like sparks of fire. It has rings or spots of color along its whole length, and can not be wounded except by shooting in the seventh spot from the head, because under this spot are its heart and its life. The blazing diamond is called Ulun'suti — "Transparent"— and he who can win it may become the greatest wonder worker of the tribe. But it is worth a man's life to attempt it, for whoever is seen by the Uktena is so dazed by the bright light that he runs toward the snake instead of trying to escape. As if this were not enough, the breath of the Uktena is so pestilential, that no living creature can survive should they inhale the tiniest bit of the foul air expelled by the Uktena. Even to see the Uktena asleep is death, not to the hunter himself, but to his family.

Daniel Brinton in his *Myths of the New World* published in 1886 explains more about the value of the horn from a horned serpent:

> The charm which [the Cherokee] presented their young men when they set out on the war path was of very similar character. It was composed of the bones of the panther and the horn of the fabulous horned snake. According to a legend taken down by an unimpeachable authority toward the close of the last century, the great snake dwelt in the waters; the old people went to the brink and sang the sacred songs. The monster rose to the surface. The sages recommenced the mystic chants. He rose a little out of the water. Again they repeated the songs. This time he showed his horns and they cut one off. Still a fourth time did they

sing, and as he rose to listen cut off the remaining horn. A fragment of these in the "war physic" protected from inimical arrows and gave success in the conflict.

In these myths, which attribute good fortune to the horn of the snake, that horn which pierces trees and rocks, which rises from the waters, which glitters as a gem, which descends from the ravines of the mountains, we shall not overstep the bounds of prudent reasoning if we see the thunderbolt, sign of the fructifying rain, symbol of the strength of the lightning, horn of the heavenly serpent. They are strictly meteorological in their meaning. And when in later Algonkin tradition the hero Michabo appears in conflict with the shining prince of serpents who lives in the lake and floods the earth with its waters, and destroys the reptile with a dart, and further when the conqueror clothes himself with the skin of his foe and drives the rest of the serpents to the south where in that latitude the lightnings are last seen in the autumn; or when in the traditional history of the Iroquois we hear of another great horned serpent rising out of the lake and preying upon the people until a similar hero-god destroys it with a thunderbolt, we cannot be wrong in rejecting any historical or ethical interpretation, and in construing them as allegories which at first represented the atmospheric changes which accompany the advancing seasons and the ripening harvests. They are narratives conveying under agreeable personifications the tidings of that unending combat which the Dakotas said was being waged with varying fortunes by Unktahe against Wauhkeon, the God of Waters against the Thunder Bird.

And he makes the point that all these dragon tales:

… are the same stories which in the old world have been elaborated into the struggles of Ormuzd and Ahriman, of

Thor and Midgard, of St. George and the Dragon, and a thousand others.

The Uktena was evil, poisonous and even the mere sight of him could cause death but if we travel to a different continent and visit South Africa, there is a completely different type of dragon. The Shangaan people tell the tale of *Masingi*, the great healer. This serpent-like dragon lived in a deep hole outside of the village in a beautiful clearing and he was known to give health to those suffering from deadly illness.

One day, a father, Khazamula fell seriously ill. His family rallied around him and tried many treatments but to no avail. Khazamula had five brave, strong sons and their mother, in fear of her husband's life, asked her children to go to Masingi, and ask for help.

Each boy, starting with the oldest, Xitetemba, went to the hole and sang to Masingi. Being way down in the hole, it was the only way to call to him. The great healing serpent heard their call and gathered his healing herbs and medicines but each time he came out, the boys grew scared and ran away. It wasn't until the youngest son, Matirhumi, sang his song and stood his ground that there was any chance of his father being healed. Matirhumi carried on singing as Masingi grew closer and allowed him to curl around his shoulders. Once the serpent was wrapped around him, Matirhumi walked home, still singing to Masingi.

Masingi healed Khazamula, staying in the village for several days to make sure his work was done. When it was time to leave, Matirhumi carried Masingi again on his shoulders, accompanied by villagers carrying gifts of thanks to the great healer. Masingi gave the young boy more healing herbs to use should his father become ill again and told him that if ever he was needed, to not be afraid but to just come and sing to him.

If we think of dragons and place, we might at first picture mountains, but from just these few short examples we already have a range of locations in which dragons dwell — from forests to

Winged dragon (on the ground). Illustration from Athanasius Kircher's *Mundus Subterraneus.*

watery ditches, and from glaciers to caves and furnaces. To further complicate matters, dragons can have four legs, two legs, or no legs at all. Some are depicted as having four wings, some two, some none. Some are like crocodiles, some are serpent-like. Some are huge sea monsters, others tiny insect-like creatures of fire. Dragons range from reptilian creatures to the roaring, fire-breathing dragons of popular Western imagination. There are dragon-carps and dragon-horses in Chinese mythology, dragon-wolfs in medieval bestiaries, part-human, part-dragon drakes in the Balkans and sparkling but evil dragons in Uzbekistan — they really come in all shapes, sizes and transfigurations!

Western dragons, for the most part, are thought of as deadly creatures; malevolent beings that should be hunted and killed. By contrast, however, Eastern cultures see the dragon as benevolent and auspicious, associated with good luck and the weather.

Across the globe dragons appear in almost every culture but their appearance, stories and meaning differ. In the following chapters we will look more closely at the myths and legends of different cultures but first let us take a tour through the evolution of the dragon through time.

Chapter 3

Early Myths

Dragons, especially those appearing as serpents or born of water, appear very early on in human history. In fact their myths and depictions are wide and varied and stem way back to possibly as far as 4000 BC. In most early myths, dragons are serpents or chimaeras but it's from these that our later legends stem.

Mesopotamia, once a historical region of southwest Asia in the Tigris and Euphrates river system and today more commonly known as Iraq, is where the earliest references to dragons or dragon-like creatures appear. In the *Epic of Gilgamesh*, Humbaba is a guardian of the Cedar Forest, where the gods lived, who is defeated by Gilgamesh and Enkidu. Humbaba is described as having the paws of a lion, a body covered in scales, with the horns of a wild bull and a snake's head at the end of his tail.

> Humbaba's roar is a flood,
> his mouth is death and his breath is fire!
> A hundred leagues away he can hear any [rustling?] in
>   his forest!
> Who would go down into his forest!

Tiamat is described in the Babylonian Epic of Creation, the *Enuma Elish*. The *Enuma Elish* is a long poem inscribed on seven tablets from c.1200 BC that tells the story of Tiamat, a primordial goddess of the sea, and Abzû, the god of fresh water, mating to produce younger gods. The tablets were found by English archaeologist, Austen Henry Layard, in 1849 in the ruined Library of Ashurbanipal at Nineveh but the myth is believed to be even older, perhaps stretching back to the start of the Mesopotamian culture in 4000 BC.

As well as a being a water goddess, Tiamat is also the monstrous embodiment of primordial chaos, sometimes appearing as a serpent or sea dragon with horns and a long tail. She gives birth to the first generation of gods who turn on their father and kill him. To avenge his death, she turns into a huge sea dragon but is slain herself by the storm god, Marduk, but not before she had birthed the first eleven monsters including a viper, a lion, a mad dog, a shark, a scorpion man, and a dragon. She is then split in two to form the earth and the sky.

A trinity of horned dragon-like creatures appear in Akkadian mythology as children of Tiamat. Bashmu, a horned snake with two forelegs and wings, Ušumgallu, the great dragon and Mušmaḫḫū, a bird-lion-serpent hybrid. On the Ishtar Gate from the city of Babylon, constructed by Nebuchadnezzar II in about 575 BC, there is another depiction of a more dog-like dragon, Mušḫuššu, made of glazed tiles.

A Mesopotamian god (with thunderbolts) battles Gryphon; often associated with the battle of Marduk versus Tiamat in the story from the *Enūma Eliš*.

In Ancient Egyptian mythology, there are several dragon or serpent-like creatures like Akhekh, Ammut, Amermait, Denwen, Nehebkau and Wadjet. Akhekh was described as a drake who lived in the wastelands and deserts and was associated with the god Seth. Some depictions are of a composite character with an antelope's body, a bird's head adorned with three uraei (snake's heads) and a long serpentine tail. Gerald Massey, in his 1881 book *A Book of the Beginnings* and his 1883 book, *The Natural Genesis*, wrote:

> One form of the Egyptian Akhekh is a Gryphon with the winged body of a beast, the tail of a serpent and head of a peacock. This is the Winged Dragon, which became the mythical Cockatrice, a compound monster having the head of a cock, the wings of a fowl, and the tail of a serpent or dragon.

The Weighing of the Heart from Ani's *The Book of the Dead*. Ammut, who will devour Ani's soul if he is unworthy, awaits the verdict.

Apep was a giant serpentine creature and deity of chaos who was the enemy of the sun god, Ra. He is likened to the myth of Tiamat and Marduk, the battle of dark and light. He lived in the underworld and was sometimes thought to be an eater of souls. Another serpent deity was Denwen who could also take the form of a dragon and held power over fire and flame. He was strong enough to destroy all of the gods with his breath of fire but was stopped by the spirit of a dead king. And then we have Ammut with the head of a crocodile, the body of a leopard and the hind quarters of a hippopotamus, known as 'The Eater of Hearts', 'The Devourer' and 'Great of Death'. If a person was found wanting when their heart was weighed on the scales of Ma'at, this deity ate them leaving their soul to wander forever.

In Zoroastrian literature from Iran and Persia, we have dragons such as Aži Dahāka, (aži meaning serpent or dragon), thought of as a human in dragon-shape or a dragon in man-shape, with three mouths, three heads and six eyes, and known for his wicked ways.

> Two maidens from the house of Jamšīd,
> were brought to him (Zahāk) like a Weeping-willow trembling,
> (maiden), who were both sisters to Jamšīd,
> (and) of the ladies were the crowns,
> of the veiled ones, one was Šahrnāz,
> and the other chaste one Arnawāz, by name,
> they were taken to the court,
> and entrusted over to the Dragon,
> who raised them in the ways of sorcery,
> (and) taught them crookedness and bad temper,
> he himself did not know better than evil teaching,
> killing, pillage, and burning.

Persian dragons were often depicted as similar to Chinese dragons with the addition of flames wrapping their bodies. Azi Sruuara was a yellow, horned dragon as big as a mountain with eyes as big as a chariot, teeth as long as a man's arm and extremely poisonous as 'over whom poison flowed the height of a spear'. He swallowed horses and men and was a highway robber! He was only killed when the hero, Kirsap, stopped to eat lunch on his back not realising he was a dragon. When he lit a fire to cook his meal, Azi Sruuara woke up and Kirsap had to run over his back for half a day until he found his head and dealt it a death blow.

Kirsap was also the hero who defeated Gandarw, a water dragon that was so big he could eat twelve men at once and was so tall that when his body was in the sea, his head reached the sun. He continually tried to devour the good things of creation and so Kirsap fought with him for nine days and nights. He managed to catch him by his golden heel and pulled his skin up from his feet to his head thus binding him. But the struggle made Kirsap so weary that he ate fifteen horses and so full was he, he fell asleep. Gandarw broke free from his bindings and taking his revenge, he pulled Kirsap's loved ones into the sea. Kirsap woke up hearing their cries and ended the life of Gandarw.

Another water dragon, Gaasyendietha, hails from Canada and Senecan mythology. The difference with this water dragon is it can leave its home in rivers and lakes and fly through the air on a trail of fire whilst also breathing out fiery jets. In more recent years, it has transformed into a more Loch Ness type of monster and taken up residence in Lake Ontario.

In North America, the Piasa bird was found as a painting on a cliff overlooking the Mississippi River north of Alton, Illinois. First seen in 1673, Father Jacques Marquette recorded on his journey down the Mississippi River that it was: '… as large as a cow with horns like a deer, red eyes, a beard like a tiger's, a face like a man. The body was covered with green, red and black scales and a tail so long it passed around the body, over the head, and between the legs'.

The story behind it was published by John Russell, a professor from a town near Alton, who believed it was a Native American bird-like dragon that devoured men. He told the story that the Piasa had

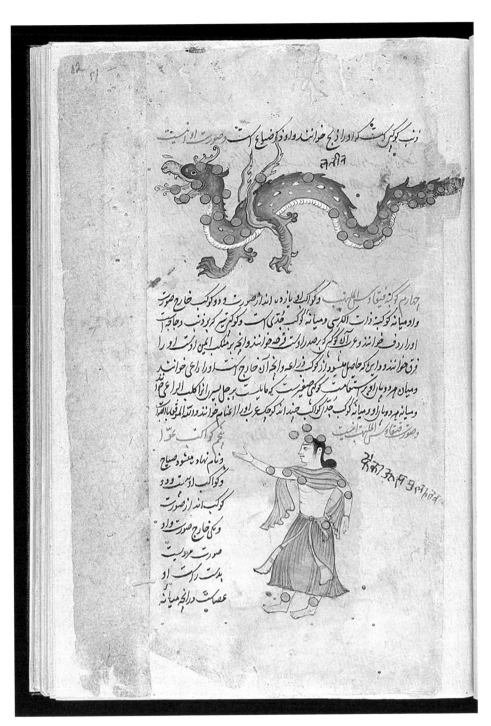

Persian miniature painting.

The Piasa bird from *Old Settler Stories*.

once terrorised the locals and had killed many of their finest warriors before it was destroyed by Chief Ouatoga's cunning plan of using himself as bait but with twenty skilled warriors hiding with poisoned arrows to ambush the creature. But it seems Russell had made the story up and no one truly knows the story behind the Piasa and who originally painted the dragon on the high cliffs of Illinois.

Other native cultures have dragon legends like the Seminole whose mythology talks of the Stvkwvnaya, a horned sea serpent. The Seminole people believed its single horn was a powerful aphrodisiac and had rituals to sing the serpent from the sea so they could harvest its horn.

In Hawaii, lizard- or dragon-like creatures up to 30 feet long called Mo'o guarded sources of freshwater and lived in pools, caves, and ponds. They could control the weather and shapeshift into seductive women, although some were male. There are many stories of the Mo'o from protectors of the land to angered dragons that could create tsunamis and needed offerings and to be honoured in order to appease them. It was said that when a Mo'o died, their bodies became a part of the landscape and helped to shape Hawaii.

The people of San Cristobal Island (now better known as Makira) of the Solomon Islands honoured Agunua (Hatuibwari) as their creator god (a male version of Mother Earth) and god of the sea. He is depicted as having a human head with four eyes, clawed arms, four breasts, large wings and the body of a serpent.

The Komodo dragon is a large species of lizard found in the Indonesian islands that still survives today and is the world's largest living lizard which can reach up to 10 feet long. Komodo dragons have no predators to compete with so they thrive and grow. Although they don't breathe fire they are known for their deadly bite. And of course legends have sprung up around them. The dragon princess of Komodo is one such tale:

Long ago a man called Empu Najo and his wife, Lea, lived on Komodo Island. Empu Najo was the leader of the village in a bay called Loh Lavi in Gili Mana, but his village often came under attack and his people would flee to the mountains, returning to their village when the threat had gone to find their goods stolen and their homes trashed. Empu Najo could see they had no future there and so he told his people they should permanently move into the mountains where they could live peacefully.

On their last night in Loh Navi, Empu Najo's wife Lea conceived. By the time she was ready to give birth the new village was finished, but there was no dukun (local doctor). Instead Empu Najo had to deliver his child. But he was surprised, shocked and frightened to find that not only did he now have a bouncing baby boy, but he also had a daughter — a daughter who had speckled, scaly skin, hooded black eyes and a tail — a daughter who in fact looked like the lizards that roamed the island.

Unfortunately Lea died and Empu Najo had to raise his children alone. He named his son Si Gerong and his daughter, Orah. They both grew up on a diet of goat's milk and honey but before long Orah was hungry for more and attacked the neighbour's chickens. Her father asked her not to feed on the villagers livestock so as she grew older she spent more and more time away from home, hunting for her own food.

Si Gerong and Orah were close but her trips home became more and more infrequent until one day she left never to return. Many years later, when Si Gerong had almost forgotten he had a sister, he went hunting in the forest on the trail of a deer. He silently crept towards it and was just about to attack when the largest dragon he had ever seen charged out of the undergrowth.

Turning to face it he raised his spear but suddenly the deer turned into a woman who said 'Put down your spear, my son. Would you kill your own sister?' The spirit of his mother told him that this was Orah and he must consider them as equals and with that she disappeared. Si Gerong and Orah stared at each other for a long time, the man and the dragon princess, before returning to their own homes. But from that day on, Si Gerong and his people always treated the dragons with kindness.

The modern-day Komodo dragon.

The Feathered Serpent deity was important in religion and depicted in the art of most of Mesoamerica and honoured by the Toltec, Olmec, Mixtec, Teotihuacan, Aztec and Mayan civilisations. His legends are complex and many, including his portrayal as a god of vegetation, rain and wind, patron of priests, and inventor of calendars and books. Known as Quetzalcoatl throughout these civilisations, he was one of four sons of the creator god Ometeotl and was responsible for creating the cosmos and giving life to men and women.

One legend tells us that Quetzalcoatl was sent to remove bones from Mictlan (the underworld) but the gods that ruled there, Lord Mictlanteuctli and Lady Mictlancihuatl, would only give them to him if Quetzalcoatl could blow a conch-shell horn that had no holes in it whilst circling the underworld four times in honour of its rulers. Not to be thwarted, Quetzalcoatl got worms to drill holes in the shell and added bees to make a sound. Mictlanteuctli reluctantly had to give up his treasured bones stating, however, that humans could not be immortal, as they one day had to return to him. But even then he could not let the bones go so he ordered the digging of a pit to entrap him.

He told Lady Mictlancihuatl that he had agreed to give Quetzalcoatl the bones but he hadn't agreed to let him leave the underworld with them. Knowing he was being tricked, Quetzalcoatl fled but still managed to fall into the pit and in doing so scattered the bones so that the male and female were mixed and broken. Quickly gathering up the bones, Quetzalcoatl escaped and fled the underworld. He took the broken bones to the great snake goddess, Cihuacoatl, who turned them into people of all shapes and sizes and thus mankind was born.

Although Quetzalcoatl is depicted as a feathered serpent, he was also able to fly and is a forerunner of later dragon legends. In more

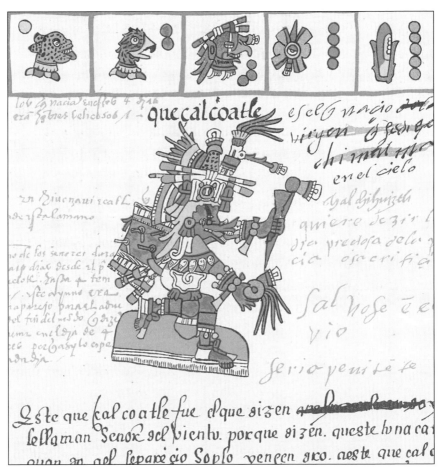

The Aztec god, Quetzalcoatl, as depicted in the *Codex Telleriano-Remensis* (16th century).

recent times, his name was used for the Pterosaur Quetzalcoatlus northropi. This flying dinosaur came in at around 10 feet tall and had a wingspan of at least 36 feet.

In the Andean civilisations of South America, the Amaru, also known as the Amaroca, Amaruca (Quechua) or Katari (Aymara) is a two-headed serpent or dragon who lives underground, or in lakes and rivers. Often depicted with one head of a bird and another a puma, Amaru is also imagined as a dragon with bird-like feet and wings.

Moving on to the European continent, there is a Basque creation myth of a serpent-like dragon in the Pyrenees. This tale tells us of Benzozia, with seven jaws and fourteen fangs, who slept beneath the earth, but she was restless and as she tossed and turned, her colourful scales pushed the earth around her, heaving it up and down, until the earth burst up from her body, forming the Pyrenees.

From her seven jaws came fire that licked over the land causing steam to rise and clouds to form. The fire then retreated, allowing water to form lakes and rivers, thus making the land fertile and allowing vegetation to grow. Soon there were trees and flowers and the earth bloomed. The fire shrank back into the earth but from its sparks came the first people, the Basque, born of Benzozia's fire.

In India the myth of Vritra and Indra was first told in the Vedic religion. In the *Rig Veda* (one of the world's oldest texts from 1500 BC), Vritra is an evil dragon and leader of the Danavas, the malevolent asuras (demons). In one version, he swallowed all the water and Indra, the king of the gods, destroyed his ninety-nine fortresses in order to defeat him and release the water: Indra's father says 'With his great thunderbolt my Son hath slaughtered Vritra and set these rivers free to wander'.

In a later version a mighty priest, Tvashtri, created a three-headed son to take over Indra's throne. Indra killed the young man with a thunderbolt and ordered that his three heads be cut off. In retaliation, Tvashtri made the dragon Vritra to destroy Indra. Vritra swallowed Indra whole but he tickled his throat until the dragon was made to vomit him out. Indra then went to the god Vishnu for advice and he was told to make peace with Vritra. This was agreed as long as Indra did not attack the dragon with a solid or liquid or attack it by day or night. Indra, however, was not content with their agreement and sought to find a way to kill Vritra. He found it at twilight which was neither night or day and he found it in a huge column of foam containing the god Vishnu that was neither solid nor liquid. The dragon was defeated but Indra's original sin of killing the priest's son was never forgiven.

Vritra trying to eat Indra.

In West African Fon creation myths the world was created by Nana-Buluku, the first primal god who gave birth to Mawu and Lisa, the sun and the moon, which are often referred to as one deity, Mawu-Lisa. She also created loa (divine spirits) to serve her, including Aido-Hwedo, a Rainbow Serpent-Dragon. The — ahem! — droppings from this dragon were used to create mountains and used as manure so that plants could grow. To stop the world from collapsing under the weight of its new growth, Aido-Hwedo offered his help by forming a large circle and biting his tail with his mouth (like the ouroboros) so encompassing the world. In doing so he grew hot so Nana-Buluku created the ocean for him so he could cool down.

Haiti and the vodou religion has a similar serpent-dragon myth. Damballah, the cosmic Rainbow Serpent is partnered with Ayida-Wedo, the Rainbow Goddess who together form divine union to create the world. Damballah is a primordial creator who used his seven thousand coils to form the universe, from the mountains and valleys to the stars and planets and from his shed skin came water. Ayida, his wife, is the goddess of the sky, fertility, rainbows, wind, water, fire, and snakes.

In Aboriginal culture we also have the Rainbow Serpent, a creator god, responsible for the land, life and water. The anthropologist, Alfred Radcliffe-Brown, coined the term Rainbow Serpent in his 1926 article 'The Rainbow-Serpent Myth of Australia' in *The Journal of the Royal Anthropological Institute of Great Britain and Ireland* which has stuck, but of course Aboriginal tribes have their own names for this creator deity and their own legends and tales that are passed down from generation to generation. There are numerous depictions in Aboriginal art of the Rainbow Serpent, some snake-like but others with chimaera aspects. For instance, a cave painting in Western Arnhem Land shows a large creature of more than 6 metres long with a dragon-like head and teeth. But why are they all strongly linked with water and the rainbow part? Well that's the serpent moving from one watering hole to another creating a prism of light as he moves.

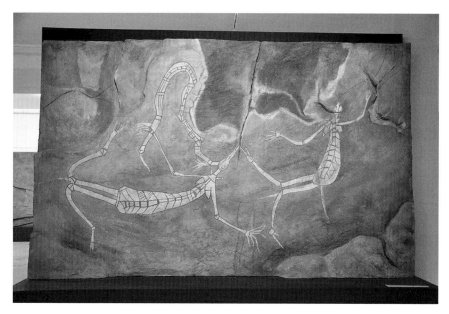

Australian Aboriginal art: Namaroto spirits and the Rainbow Serpent, Burlung.

One widespread story tells of the Wawalag, or Wagilag, sisters who were travelling together towards the Arafura Sea. The older sister, heavily pregnant, eventually gave birth and her blood flowed down into a waterhole, where the Rainbow Serpent lived. The Rainbow Serpent smelt the blood and followed it back to the sisters, asleep in their hut, and then ate them up whole. However, the Rainbow Serpent was bitten by an ant which made him vomit up the sisters. Their bodies turned to stone and helped create the landscape of Arnhem Land.

Then there are more local stories like that of the Kanmare, a huge supernatural water-snake with a mane around its head, in the Boulia district of Queensland, also known as Tulloun by the Mitakoodi people. If a man is fishing by the water, unknowing to him, Kanmare will point a 'death-bone' at him. Soon he will see the Kanmare undulating beneath the surface of the water and he will run for home. He will then fall sick for four or five days until a doctor is called to cut a stone, pebble, flint or bone out of the man. This stone is actually the same bone Kanmare pointed at the man. When the man recovers, he will become a doctor.

Maori legends tell of the Taniwha — supernatural creatures similar to serpents and dragons — who hide in rivers, lakes, caves or the sea. Some Taniwha are evil creatures who kill people but others are guardians and protectors. One Taniwha, Tūtaeporoporo, began life as a shark before he was caught by a chief and kept as a pet in a river. The more time Tūtaeporoporo spent there, the more he changed into a dragon, growing scaly skin, webbed feet, wings, and a bird-like head. Then he got hungry so he started eating people until Ao-kehu, a Taniwha slayer, hid inside a hollow log to await his prey. Tūtaeporoporo could smell him there so he swallowed the log whole with Ao-kehu inside. Ao-kehu fought back, slicing and stabbing until he was free from the Taniwha's stomach, who now weakened, was easy to kill.

So from the earliest myths we have dragons as serpents or with bird-like attributes, lion paws, horns, wings, reptilian skin. They morph and change between countries and continents, but their stories are an essential and integral part of the lives and cultures of the people who told them.

Taniwha rock carving, part of modern Maori rock carvings on Lake Taupo.

Chapter 4

From the Ancient World to Classical Civilisations

Moving on from early creation myths we now come to the classic civilisations of Greece and Rome. The English word 'dragon' comes from the Greek word 'drakon' meaning huge serpent. The dragon at this stage was still very much serpent-like although we also have chimaeras, the concept of fire-breathing and the powers of dragon teeth.

Ancient Greek mythology is vivid, rich and diverse, and well-documented allowing us to read many translated primary sources. Within the numerous tales fall different types of dragon. First we have the serpentine Dracones or dragon-serpents that pulled Medea's flying chariot through the sky. Medea was the granddaughter of the sun god, Helios, most famous for helping Jason retrieve the golden fleece.

> She [Medea, posing as a priestess of Artemis,] declared [to King Pelias] that Artemis, riding through the air upon a chariot drawn by Drakones (dragon-serpents), had flown in the air over many parts of the inhabited earth and had chosen the realm of the most pious king in all the world for the establishment of her own worship and for honours which should be for ever and ever … By means of certain drugs, Medea caused shapes of Drakones to appear, which she declared had brought the goddess through the air from the Hyperboreans to make her stay with Pelias.

Then we have the Cetea (Ketea) who were large sea creatures, monsters of the sea and often depicted as giant serpents with long rows of sharp teeth:

67. *Trucidatis liberis Medea fugam capeßit.*

Medea destroying Jason's family and home, from Ovid's *Metamorphoses*.

The Ketea, mighty of limb and huge, the wonders of the sea, heavy with strength invincible, a terror for the eyes to behold and ever armed with deadly rage — many of these thee be that roam the spacious seas, where are the unmapped prospects of Poseidon, but few of them come night the shore, those only whose weight the beaches can bear and whom the salt water does not fail.

Among these are the terrible Lion and the truculent Hammer-head and the deadly Leopard and the dashing Physalos (sperm-whale); among them also is the impetuous black race of the Tunny and the deadly Saw-fish and the dread gave of the woeful Lamna and the Maltha, named not from soft feebleness, and the terrible Ramas and the awful weight of the Hyaena, and the ravenous and shameless Dog-fish. Of the Dog-fish there are three races; one fierce race in the deep seas is numbered among the terrible Ketea (Cetea, Sea-Monsters); two other races among the mightiest fishes dwell in the deep mud.

The Cetea appear in several stories including that of Andromeda. Andromeda was the daughter of King Cepheus and Queen Cassiopeia, king and queen of the kingdom Aethiopia. Queen Cassiopeia one day boasted that her daughter was more beautiful than the Nereids, the sea nymphs, which angered Poseidon greatly. He sent the sea monster, Cetus, to ravage the coast of Aethiopia causing havoc and destruction. The king and queen did not know how to appease him so King Cepheus consulted the Oracle of Apollo, who told them that the only way to quell the raging beast was to sacrifice their daughter, Andromeda, to him. She was chained to a rock in the sea as sacrifice but Perseus, who was returning from having slain the Gorgon Medusa, saw her there. Made invisible by Hades' helm, he killed the sea monster. In one version, he uses Medusa's head to turn the Cetus to stone, whilst in another he stabs him in the back. Andromeda was then freed and as heroes are wont to do, Perseus married her.

Next we have the fire-breathing Chimaera, a female monster of different parts, with the body and head of a lion, a goat's head rising from her back, the udders of a goat, and a snake for a tail. King Iobates of Lycia commanded the hero, Bellerophon, to kill her for she was scorching his land with flame:

> He ordered Bellerophon to slay the Khimaira [Chimaera], assuming that he would instead be destroyed himself by the beast, since not even a quantity of men could subdue it with ease, let alone one. For it was a single being that had the force of three beasts, the front part of a lion, the tail of a drakon, and the third (middle) head was that of a goat, through which it breathed out fire. It despoiled the countryside and ravaged the herds. It was allegedly

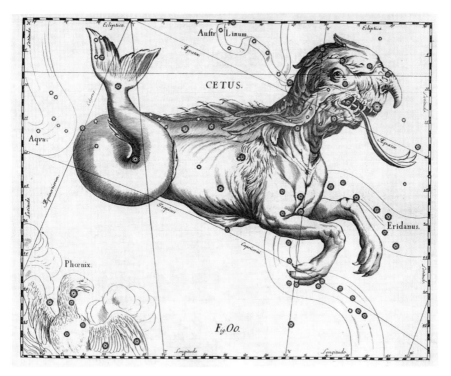

The Cetus constellation from *Uranographia* by Johannes Hevelius.

reared by Amisodaros [Amisodarus], as Homer also states, and according to Hesiod its parents were Typhon and Ekhidna [Echidna]. Bellerophon mounted Pegasos [Pegasus], his winged horse born of Medousa [Medusa] and Poseidon, and flying high into the air brought down the Khimaira with his bow and arrows.

Another female dragon is the Scythian Dracaena who was a woman from the waist up with the tail of a serpent instead of legs.

Medea appears again in the story of the Colchian Dragon, who was a giant serpent that guarded the Golden Fleece in the sacred grove. When Jason and the Argonauts went to fetch the fleece, the dragon was killed by Jason in one interpretation but in another was put to sleep by Medea. Another story depicted on a vase, shows Jason being eaten by the dragon but then vomited up — a re-occurring theme as we have seen.

Chimaera on a red-figure Apulian plate, c.350–340 BCE.

The dragon's teeth were harvested for their magical properties by King Aeetes who ordered that Jason should plant them in a sacred field belonging to the war-god, Ares, with a plough drawn by fire-breathing bulls. When they grew, they developed as humans, named the Spartoi (literally sown men), who were a tribe of warlike, earth-born men.

Dragon's teeth also feature in the legends of the Phoenician prince, Cadmus, who fought the dragon of Ares.

> Kadmos [Cadmus] sent some of his men to fetch water
> from the spring of Ares, but a Serpent, said by some to be
> a child of Ares, guarded the spring and destroyed most of
> those who had been sent. In outrage Kadmos killed the

Serpent, and then, following the instructions of Athena, planted its teeth. From this sowing there sprang from the earth armed men, called Spartoi ... As for Kadmos, to atone for the deaths he served Ares as a labourer for an 'everlasting year,' for a year then was equal to eight years now. After his period of labour, Athena provided Kadmos with the sovereignty [of Thebes], and Zeus gave him Harmonia, daughter of Aphrodite and Ares, as a wife.

As well as flying serpents, guardians and life givers, dragons were also slain regularly by Greek heroes — the most famous being Heracles who fought the Lernaean Hydra, a humongous nine-headed water-serpent. Heracles had to destroy her as one of his twelve labours, but it was no easy task:

For his second labour, Herakles [Heracles] was instructed to slay the Lernaian [Lernaean] Hydra. The beast was

Cadmus slays the dragon.

nurtured in the marshes of Lerna, from where she would go out onto the flatland to raid flocks and ruin the land. The Hydra was of enormous size, with eight mortal heads, and a ninth one in the middle that was immortal. With Iolaos [Iolaus] driving, Herakles rode a chariot to Lerna, and there, stopping the horses, he found the Hydra on a ridge beside the springs of Amymone where she nested. By throwing flaming spears at her he forced her to emerge, and as she did he was able to catch hold. But she hung on to him by wrapping herself round one of his feet, and he was unable to help matters by striking her with his club, for as soon as one head was pounded off two others would grow in its place. Then a giant crab came along to help the Hydra, and bit Herakles on the foot. For this he killed the crab and called on his own behalf to Iolaos for help. Iolaos made some torches by setting fire to a portion of the adjoining woods, and, by using these to burn the buddings of the heads, he kept them from growing. When he had overcome this problem, Herakles lopped off the immortal head, which he buried and covered with a heavy boulder at the side of the road that runs through Lerna to Elaios [Elaeus]. He cut up the Hydra's body and dipped his arrows in its venom.

Zeus, the god of the sky and lightning and the father of all gods and goddesses, battled the monster Typhon, a man from the waist up but with two coiled serpents instead of legs:

Typhon was a mixture of man and beast, the largest and strongest of all Ge's [Earth's] children. Down to the thighs he was human in form, so large that he extended beyond all the mountains while his head often touched even the stars. One hand reached to the west, the other to the east, and attached to these were one hundred heads of serpents. Also from the thighs down he had great coils of vipers, which extended to the top of his head and hissed mightily. All of his body was winged, and the hair that flowed in the wind from his head and cheeks was matted and dirty. In his eyes flashed fire. Such were the appearance and the size of Typhon as he hurled red-hot rocks at the sky itself and set out for it with mixed hisses and shouts, as a great storm of fire boiled forth from his mouth.

Zeus managed to defeat Typhon by hurling his lightning bolt at him. Some stories say Typhon was returned to Tartarus from whence he had come but others say he was imprisoned under Mount Etna or Vesuvius. Typhon's fiery breath became an explanation for why volcanoes bubble up hot lava; and his rage sometimes forces them to erupt.

Before Typhon was defeated, he had children with Echidna, another dragon prototype who was half-woman, half-snake. Their offspring included the Hydra of Lerna and the Chimaera as mentioned above but also Cerberus. We know Cerberus to be a three-headed dog or hellhound that guarded the entrance to Hades, the underworld of the dead, but according to Apollodorus, Cerberus also had a dragon or serpent tail and snake heads all over his back — not surprising given his mother and father were also part-snake!

Laocoon was a Trojan priest who along with his two sons was attacked by serpents (yet more offspring of Typhon) that had been sent by the war goddess Athena. Laocoon had dared to try to stop the fall of Troy:

Laokoon [Laocoon] wisely he spake: 'A deadly fraud is this [the Wooden Horse],' he said, 'devised by the Akhaian chiefs!' And cried to all straightway to burn the Horse, and know if aught within its timbers lurked. Yea, and they had obeyed him, and had 'scaped destruction; but Athena, fiercely wroth with him, the Trojans, and their city, shook earth's deep foundations 'neath Laokoon's feet.

Tornado–Zeus Battling Typhon, from Erasmus Darwin's *The Botanic Garden.*

Straight terror fell on him, and trembling bowed the knees of the presumptuous: round his head horror of darkness poured; a sharp pang thrilled his eyelids; swam his eyes beneath his brows; his eyeballs, stabbed with bitter anguish, throbbed even from the roots, and rolled in frenzy of pain. Clear through his brain the bitter torment pierced even to the filmy inner veil thereof; now bloodshot were his eyes, now ghastly green; anon with rheum they ran, as pours a stream down from a rugged crag, with thawing snow made turbid. As a man distraught he seemed: all things he saw showed double, and he groaned fearfully; yet he ceased not to exhort the men of Troy, and recked not of his pain. Then did the Goddess strike him utterly blind. Stared his fixed eyeballs white from pits of blood; and all folk groaned for pity of their friend, and dread of the Prey-giver, lest he had sinned in folly against her, and his mind was thus warped to destruction yea, lest on themselves like judgment should be visited, to avenge the outrage done to hapless Sinon's flesh, whereby they hoped to wring the truth from him. So led they him in friendly wise to Troy, pitying him at the last.

Then gathered all, and o'er that huge Horse hastily cast a rope, and made it fast above; for under its feet smooth wooden rollers had Epeios laid, that, dragged by Trojan hands, it might glide on into their fortress … Grimly Enyo laughed, seeing the end of that dire war; Hera rejoiced on high; glad was Athena. When the Trojans came unto their city, brake they down the walls, their city's coronal, that the Horse of Death might be led in. Troy's daughters greeted it with shouts of salutation; marvelling all gazed at the mighty work where lurked their doom.

Laokoon (despite being struck blind by Athena) ceased not to exhort his countrymen to burn the Horse with fire: they would not hear, for dread of the Gods' wrath. But then a yet more hideous punishment Athena visited on his hapless sons. A cave there was, beneath a rugged cliff exceeding high, unscalable, wherein dwelt fearful monsters of the deadly brood of Typhon, in the rock-clefts of the isle Kalydna that looks Troyward from the sea. Thence stirred she up the strength of serpents twain, and summoned them to Troy. By her uproused they shook the island as with earthquake: roared the sea; the waves disparted as they came. Onward they swept with fearful-flickering tongues …

Swiftly they came whither the Goddess sped them: with grim jaws whetting their deadly fangs, on his hapless sons sprang they. All Trojans panic-stricken fled, seeing those fearsome Drakones in their town. No man, though ne'er so dauntless theretofore, dared tarry; ghastly dread laid hold on all shrinking in horror from the monsters. Screamed the women; yea, the mother forgat her child, fear-frenzied as she fled: all Troy became one shriek of fleers, one huddle of jostling limbs: the streets were choked with cowering fugitives. Alone was left Laokoon with his sons, for death's doom and the Goddess chained their feet. Then, even as from destruction shrank the lads, those deadly fangs had seized and ravined up the twain, outstretching to their sightless sire agonized hands: no power to help had he. Trojans far off looked on from every side weeping, all dazed. And, having now fulfilled upon the Trojans Pallas' awful hest, those monsters vanished 'neath the earth; and still stands their memorial, where into the fane they entered of Apollon in Pergamos the hallowed.

The Romans mostly adapted Greek myths to continue the dragon legends rather than creating their own. However, dragons were very much a part of their mythology. In chapter one we mentioned the dragon of the Bagrada river that attacked the Roman army and whose body was sent back to Rome.

Regulus, chosen by lot for the Carthaginian War, marched with his army to a point not far from the Bagrada River and there pitched his camp. In that place a reptile of astonishing size devoured many of the soldiers as they went down to the river to get water. Regulus set out with his army to attack the reptile. Neither the javelins they hurled nor the darts they rained upon its back had any effect. These glided off its horrible scaly fins as if from a slanting testudo of shields and were in some miraculous fashion turned away from its body so that the creature suffered no injury.

Finally, when Regulus saw that it was killing a great number of his soldiers with its bites, was trampling them down by its charge, and driving them mad by its poisonous breath, he ordered ballistae brought up. A stone taken from a wall was hurled by a ballista; this struck the spine of the serpent and caused its entire body to become numb. The formation of the reptile was such that, though it seemed to lack feet, yet it had ribs and scales graded evenly, extending from the top of its throat to the lowest part of its belly and so arranged that the creature rested upon its scales as if on claws and upon its ribs as if on legs.

But it did not move like the worm which has a flexible spine and moves by first stretching its contracted parts in the direction of its tiny body and then drawing together the stretched parts. This reptile made its way by a sinuous movement, extending its sides first right and then left, so that it might keep the line of ribs rigid along the exterior arch of the spine; nature fastened the claws of its scales to its ribs, which extend straight to their highest point; making these moves alternately and quickly, it not only glided over levels, but also mounted inclines, taking as many footsteps, so to speak, as it had ribs.

This is why the stone rendered the creature powerless. If struck by a blow in any part of the body from its bowels to its head, it is crippled and unable to move, because wherever the blow falls, it numbs the spine, which stimulates the feet of the ribs and the motion of the body. Hence this serpent, which had for a long time withstood so many javelins unharmed, moved about disabled from the blow of a single stone and, quickly overcome by spears, was easily destroyed. Its skin was brought to Rome — it is said to have been one hundred and twenty feet in length — and for some time was an object of wonder to all.

Battling dragons was obviously a good excuse for failure! Although in this case the creature was more than likely a giant anaconda or python. The Romans, however, did believe in the strength and might of the dragon. Around the 2nd century AD, the Roman military used the draco, a dragon's head mounted on a staff with brightly coloured cloth trailing from it, as the standard for a cohort which was carried by the draconarius or standard bearer.

A dragon in a landscape, which, according to the Italian inscription, lived in the swamps outside Rome

We also have the folktale of the mud dragon who lived in the mud pits outside a prosperous city. He defended the city from its enemies but it came with a price. Once a month a virgin had to take him a basket of food and feed him by hand. If he felt she was impure, he ate her too. However, if she was of strong and pure heart he allowed her to return to the city.

And although the Romans continued many of the Greek legends, dragons and the like would continue in their literature and poetry. Vergil's poem *The Gnat* describes a snake that seems somewhat like a dragon:

> By paths the same, a monstrous speckled snake
> With many-coloured body now there comes
> To sink submerged in mud I' th'heat intense.
> With brassy coat 'twas heavy, snapping at
> Whate'er was in the way with quiv'ring tongue,
> And twirled its scaly coils with motions wide.

The gleams of it approaching took upon
Themselves fantastic shapes at every point.
Now curving more and more a body which
Is capable of bending back it lifts
Its breast with shining splendours, and upon
Th'uplifted neck the head itself, from which
A crest is upwards raised: conspicuous
With purple hood 'tis variegated all,
And from its savage glare there gleams the flash
Of flames.

Chapter 5

Viking Dragons

The Vikings loved their 'dreki' — sea monsters, sea serpents, and dragons — who featured in prominent stories from Norse mythology but they also used the symbolism of the dragon to denote strength, bravery, destructive power, violence, chaos and death. Carved wooden dragons could be found on buildings probably as a form of protection and depicted on runestones, jewellery and in art. Dragon heads were also used on longships as a warning that trouble was coming and removed if the incoming boat was peaceful.

And, as in this poem by Rasmus Björn Anderson, these ships themselves were described as dragon-like:

Carved dragon head.

Dragon-shap'd it lay on the sea; fall high o'er the waters
Rose its proud head, while its wide throat flam'd, with
  red gold thickly cover'd;
Speckled with yellow and blue was the belly; but back
  toward the rudder
Curv'd its strong-knit tail in a ring, all scaly with silver.
Black were its wings, with edgings of gold; when each
  one was full-stretch'd.

There are three main dragons in Norse mythology. Jormungandr or the 'Midgard Serpent' was a dragon that encompassed the world or Midgard. Like our other cosmic dragons, he was more serpent-like and lived in the waters of earth but was so enormous that his body could wrap around it so his head could bite his tail like an ouroboros — an ancient symbol that represents the cycle of birth and death. He was one of the three children born to Loki, the trickster god, and the giantess Angrboda, along with Hel, goddess of the underworld and Fenrir, the giant wolf.

Thor, the god of thunder and son of Odin, was his sworn enemy. Thor and Jormungandr's father, Loki, once travelled to the land of giants, Utgard-Loki. There they were taunted because they were so small and puny. Angered, Thor agreed to take part in tests to prove his might. The king of Utgard-Loki told him to lift up a cat in his great hall. Thor wasn't bothered with such a simple task but when he tried with all his might he could only get one paw off the ground. What he didn't know was that the cat was actually Jormungandr, the Midgard Serpent, in disguise. And what he had actually managed was an impressive feat, for Jormungandr was so tightly wrapped around the world that even to lift a tiny part of him was an act of strength but also a very dangerous deed that might cause the world to flood.

Jormungandr lived partially in the sea and he would meet Thor again when Thor went fishing with the giant Hymir. Hymir wouldn't

Thor battering the Midgard Serpent (1790).

give Thor any bait, so he chopped off the head of the giant's largest ox to use. They rowed out to sea but Thor urged Hymir to row further to find just the right spot. There he baited his line with the ox head, which attracted one hungry serpent — Jormungandr. As Thor pulled him from the water, Jormungandr blew poison in his face. As Hymir began to panic, Thor grabbed his hammer to deal Jormungandr a death blow but the giant severed the line and our serpent-like dragon escaped back into the depths. Some stories tell that Thor did indeed kill Jormungandr but he appears again at Ragnarok, the end of the world of gods and men.

Retold in the *Prose Edda* and in a single poem in the *Poetic Edda*, Ragnarok is the 'Twilight of the Gods'. It is prophesised that the world tree, Yggdrasil, that holds the cosmos together, will fall. Fenrir, the monstrous wolf, will run free and Jormungandr will rise from the depths of the sea, raising water over all the earth as he lands ashore and his mouth and tail come apart to unleash torrents across the globe. Fighting will commence with, amongst others, Fenrir killing Odin and then being killed by his son Vidar, and Thor and Jormungandr will have their final battle. The serpent-dragon will spew poison at the god of thunder but be struck down. Thor will only get nine paces away before he is overcome by venomous fumes and perishes also.

Yggdrasil also features as the home of another dragon. Vǫluspá (Prophecy of the Seeress) is the best known poem of the tenth century *Poetic Edda*, a collection of old narrative poems. It tells the story of the creation of the nine realms of Norse cosmology that are joined by the world tree. Níðhöggr or Nidhogg is a winged dragon who gnaws at the roots of Yggdrasil, threatening the balance of the worlds and the downfall of the gods. He is a symbol of decay, loss of honour and villainy and one of the harbingers of Ragnarok.

One story tells that while Nidhogg can be found in the roots of Yggdrasil, a wise eagle lives high in the branches at the top of the tree. They despise each other and it is made worse by Ratatoskr, the tricky squirrel, who runs up and down the trunk of the tree spurring on their hatred by spreading lies and making up insults they had supposedly thrown at each other.

> Ratatosks [Ratatoskr] is the squirrel who there shall run
> on the ash-tree Yggdrasil;
> from above the words of the eagle he bears,
> and tells them to Nithhogg beneath.

Nidhogg becomes increasingly offended and vows to kill the eagle, but he is so furious that he shakes the tree so hard and the nine realms tremble, setting him free of Yggdrasil's roots. His release will signal the coming of Ragnarok, the end of the world.

Dronke's translation tells us:

> A hall she saw standing
> remote from the sun
> on Dead Body Shore.
> Its door looks north.
> There fell drops of venom
> in through the roof vent.
> That hall is woven
> of serpents' spines.
> She saw there wading
> onerous streams
> men perjured
> and wolfish murderers
> and the one who seduces
> another's close-trusted wife.
> There Malice Striker sucked
> corpses of the dead,
> the wolf tore men.
> Do you still seek to know? And what?

The Nordic trio of Urðr, Verðandi and Skuld beneath the world tree, Yggdrasil. At the top of the tree is an eagle (likely Veðrfölnir), on the trunk of the tree is a squirrel (likely Ratatoskr), and at the roots of the tree gnaws what appears to be a small dragon (likely Níðhöggr).

Nidhogg is 'Malice striker' or 'he who strikes with malice', the chaos-bringer who is malicious and evil. A later tale says that he resides in Nástrǫnd (Corpse Shore), a place in Niflheim ruled by the goddess Hel, where he lives and chews on corpses. It is an underworld for those guilty of murder, adultery, and oath-breaking and who apparently make tasty snacks!

> There comes the shadowy
> dragon flying,
> glittering serpent, up
> from Dark of the Moon Hills.
> He carries in his pinions
> — he flies over the field —
> Malice Striker, corpses.
> Now will she sink.

The *Prose Edda* also refers to Nidhogg as a dragon who gnaws at one of the three roots of Yggdrasil, the world tree, because the roots are actually trapping him. Nidhogg is mentioned in a list of serpents that include Goin, Moin, Grafvitnir, Grabak, Ofnir, Svafnir and Fafnir.

Fafnir was also a serpent-like dragon with no wings and no fire. Fafnir was once a dwarf but he grew too greedy. His father, Hreithmar, received a hoard of gold from Loki (other tales say Odin) in repayment for the loss of one of his sons. Fafnir coveted the gold and murdered his father to possess it without knowing there was a curse upon it. Then he turned into a dragon to guard his hoard. If that makes you think of Smaug in *The Hobbit*, you would be right! Tolkien drew on many stories including that of Fafnir to create Smaug.

There's also a ring in the golden horde. Andvaranaut is a magic ring that helps the owner to find gold. The ring and the treasure once belonged to Andvari, a dwarf that can change himself into a pike, until Loki stole it.

Fafnir was later slain by the young hero, Sigurd, the son of King Sigmund, spurred on by the blacksmith, Regin, (who was actually Fafnir's brother). Twice a sword was made and twice it was broken until Regin re-forged the mighty sword Gram, for Sigurd to use as a weapon.

Of the Slaying of the Worm Fafnir

Now Sigurd and Regin ride up the heath along that same way wherein Fafnir was wont to creep when he fared to the water; and folk say that thirty fathoms was the height of that cliff along which he lay when he drank of the water below. Then Sigurd spake:

‘How sayedst thou, Regin, that this drake was no greater than other lingworms; methinks the track of him is marvellous great?’

Then said Regin, ‘Make thee a hole, and sit down therein, and whenas the worm comes to the water, smite him into the heart, and so do him to death, and win thee great fame thereby.’ But Sigurd said, ‘What will betide me if I be before the blood of the worm?’ Says Regin, ‘Of what avail to counsel thee if thou art still afeard of everything? Little art thou like thy kin in stoutness of heart.’

Then Sigurd rides right over the heath; but Regin gets him gone, sore afeard.

But Sigurd fell to digging him a pit, and whiles he was at that work, there came to him an old man with a long beard, and asked what he wrought there, and he told him.

Then answered the old man and said, ‘Thou doest after sorry counsel: rather dig thee many pits, and let the blood run therein; but sit thee down in one thereof, and so thrust the worm’s heart through.’

And therewithal he vanished away; but Sigurd made the pits even as it was shown to him.

Now crept the worm down to his place of watering, and the earth shook all about him, and he snorted forth venom on all the way before him as he went; but Sigurd neither trembled nor was adrad at the roaring of him. So whenas the worm crept over the pits, Sigurd thrust his sword under his left shoulder, so that it sank in up to the hilts; then up leapt Sigurd from the pit and drew the sword back again unto him, and therewith was his arm all bloody, up to the very shoulder.

Now when that mighty worm was ware that he had his death-wound, then he lashed out head and tail, so that all things soever that were before him were broken to pieces.

So whenas Fafnir had his death-wound, he asked 'Who art thou? And who is thy father? And what thy kin, that thou wert so hardy as to bear weapons against me?'

Sigurd answered, 'Unknown to men is my kin. I am called a noble beast: neither father have I nor mother, and all alone have I fared hither.'

Said Fafnir, 'Whereas thou hast neither father nor mother, of what wonder weft thou born then? But now, though thou tellest me not thy name on this my death-day, yet thou knowest verily that thou liest unto me.'

He answered, 'Sigurd am I called, and my father was Sigmund.'

Says Fafnir, 'Who egged thee on to this deed, and why wouldst thou be driven to it? Hadst thou never heard how that all folk were adrad of me, and of the awe of my countenance? But an eager father thou hadst, O bright eyed swain!'

Sigurd answered, 'A hardy heart urged me on hereto, and a strong hand and this sharp sword, which well thou knowest now, stood me in stead in the doing of the deed. "Seldom hath hardy eld a faint-heart youth."'

Fafnir said, 'Well, I wot that hadst thou waxed amid thy kin, thou mightest have good skill to slay folk in thine anger; but more of a marvel is it, that thou, a bondsman taken in war, shouldst have the heart to set on me, "for few among bondsmen have heart for the fight."'

Said Sigurd, 'Wilt thou then cast it in my teeth that I am far away from my kin? Albeit I was a bondsman, yet was I never shackled. God wot thou hast found me free enow.' Fafnir answered, 'In angry wise dost thou take my speech; but hearken, for that same gold which I have owned shall be thy bane too.'

Quoth Sigurd, 'Fain would we keep all our wealth til that day of days; yet shall each man die once for all.'

Said Fafnir, 'Few things wilt thou do after my counsel, but take heed that thou shalt be drowned if thou farest unwarily over the sea; so bide thou rather on the dry land for the coming of the calm tide.'

Then said Sigurd, 'Speak, Fafnir, and say, if thou art so exceeding wise, who are the Norns who rule the lot of all mothers' sons.'

Fafnir answers, 'Many there be and wide apart; for some are of the kin of the Aesir, and some are of Elfin kin, and some there are who are daughters of Dvalin.'

Said Sigurd, 'How namest thou the holm whereon Surt and the Aesir mix and mingle the water of the sword?'

'Unshapen is that holm hight,' said Fafnir.

And yet again he said, 'Regin, my brother, has brought about my end, and it gladdens my heart that thine too he bringeth about; for thus will things be according to his will.'

And once again he spake, 'A countenance of terror I bore up before all folk, after that I brooded over the heritage of my brother, and on every side did I spout out poison, so that none durst come anigh me, and of no weapon was I adrad, nor ever had I so many men before me, as that I deemed myself not stronger than all; for all men were sore afeard of me.'

Sigurd answered and said, 'Few may have victory by means of that same countenance of terror, for whoso comes amongst many shall one day find that no one man is by so far the mightiest of all.'

Then says Fafnir, 'Such counsel I give thee, that thou take thy horse and ride away at thy speediest, for ofttimes it fails out so, that he who gets a death-wound avenges himself none the less.'

Sigurd answered, 'Such as thy redes are I will nowise do after them; nay, I will ride now to thy lair and take to me that great treasure of thy kin.'

'Ride there then,' said Fafnir, 'and thou shalt find gold enow to suffice thee for all thy life-days; yet shall that gold be thy bane, and the bane of every one soever who owns it.'

Then up stood Sigurd, and said, 'Home would I ride and lose all that wealth, if I deemed that by the losing thereof I should never die; but every brave and true man will fain have his hand on wealth till that last day that thou, Fafnir, wallow in the death-pain til Death and Hell have thee.'

And therewithal Fafnir died.

Back at camp, Regin asked Sigurd to cook the dragon's heart for him. As Sigurd was cooking it on the fire he burnt his thumb on the heart. Putting it in his mouth to soothe the pain, he realised he could now understand the language of birds. The birds warned him that Regin was going to kill him, so Sigurd killed the blacksmith and took Fafnir's treasure for himself.

Sigurd is arguably the most famous of Norse dragon slayers but there are others including Ragnar Lothbrok, made famous by the Vikings TV series. In the sagas, Ragnar is the son of King Sigurd Hring of Sweden, and leader of raids in England and Europe. In the Danish *Gesta Danorum* ('deeds of the Danes'), written by Saxo Grammaticus in the thirteenth century, Ragnar's story is recounted. Ragnar had divorced his wife, Lagertha, and was enamoured with Thora Borgarhjört, daughter of King Herraud, Earl of Götaland. The only problem was she had two lindworms that her father had given her to raise after he found them one day whilst out hunting. They had

Siegfried (Sigurd) kills the dragon Fafnir.

grown in size and were now causing havoc with their pestilential breath, so Herraud decided whoever killed the beasts would get his daughter in marriage.

Ragnar, learning from men who travelled to and fro how the matter stood, asked his nurse for a woollen mantle, and for some thigh-pieces that were very hairy, with which he could repel the snake bites. He thought that he ought to use a dress stuffed with hair to protect himself, and also took one that was not unwieldy, that he might move nimbly. And when he had landed in Sweden, he deliberately plunged his body in water, while there was a frost falling, and, wetting his dress, to make it the less penetrable, he let the cold freeze it. Thus attired, he took leave of his companions, exhorted them to remain loyal to Fridleif, and went on to the palace alone. When he saw it, he tied his sword to his side, and lashed a spear to his right hand with a thong. As he went on, an enormous snake glided up and met him. Another, equally huge, crawled up, following in the trail of the first. They strove now to buffet the young man with the coils of their tails, and now to spit and belch their venom stubbornly upon him.

He was laughed at for his unusual dress (trousers) and given the nickname Loðbrók (Old Icelandic for 'hairy-trousers' or 'shaggy-breeches') but Ragnar, trusting in the hardness of his frozen dress, foiled the poisonous assaults not only with his arms, but with his attire, and, single-handed, in unweariable combat, stood up against the two gaping creatures, who stubbornly poured forth their venom upon him. For their teeth he repelled with his shield, their poison with his dress. At last he cast his spear, and drove it against the bodies of the brutes, who were fiercely attacking him. He pierced both their hearts, and his battle ended in victory. And of course Ragnar won his bride and went on to have sons, Eric and Agnar. Although there's no mention of how Thora felt about him having killed her pets!

Dragons also appear in other tales including that of the fifteenth-century Icelandic romance *Sigrgarðs saga frækna* [the saga of Sigrgarðr the Valiant] translated by Hall, Richardson and Þorgeirsson. This time we have more of a vanquishing rather than dragon slaying.

In summary, Knútr killed a witch and on investigating her dwelling found a dragon living underneath it. He blew poison that he had found in the witch's bag on the creature and it flew out of the window. And what had he been guarding? Gold treasure! Knútr took the gold and made his escape but as he sailed away the dragon reared out of the water and attacked his boat. He fought back, smashing the beast on the nose but it still took the boat down. Knútr jumped onto the dragon's back and wrestled with it until he was closer to shore. Then he used the magic dust again, sprinkling it all over the wounded creature. Now weakened, it began to sink down to the depths and Knútr was able to make his way to land.

Dragons were not just a revered creature of the Vikings of course. They began to feature heavily in medieval stories and art and as the Middle Ages progressed, stories of these magnificent beasts became more and more popular. But the rise of Christianity would mean tales of the dragon would eventually take a dark turn.

Chapter 6

Christianity and the Dragon

The Spanish theologian, Isidore of Seville, wrote a chapter on snakes and dragons in chapter IV of Book XII of his *Etymologiae*. Echoing Pliny and his discussion of dragons and elephants, Isidore of Seville wrote:

> The dragon is the largest of all the snakes, or of all the animals on earth. The Greeks call it Δράκων, whence the term is borrowed into Latin so that we say draco. It is often drawn out of caves and soars aloft, and disturbs the air. Even the elephant with his huge body is not safe from the dragon, for it lurks around the paths along which the elephants are accustomed to walk, and wraps around their legs in coils and kills them by suffocating them.

He also noted that snakes were always considered among pagans as the spirits of place. To equate the dragon with pagans at a time when Christianity was spreading across the globe meant their stories would now change. As Christianity spread, so too did the notion of what dragons symbolise. Rather than being a creature from creation myths or moral tales, lauded and honoured, their reputation now took a dive and they were seen negatively as characters in a war between light and dark forces, in a battle between good and evil.

Hugh of Fouilloy, author of the *De avibus*, the Medieval Book of Birds, said:

> The dragon, the greatest of all serpents, is the devil, the king of all evil. As it deals death with its poisonous breath

and blow of its tail, so the devil destroys men's souls by thought, word, and deed.

We still have our fire-breathing, poisonous breath and/or immense tail but with Christianity the dragon became the enemy and the bible had several stories to underline its darkness as in *The Book of Revelation* (12:1, 3-4):

> Then another sign appeared in heaven: an enormous red dragon with seven heads and ten horns and seven crowns on its heads. Its tail swept a third of the stars out of the sky and flung them to the earth. The dragon stood in

Dragon and elephant (from a medieval bestiary).

front of the woman who was about to give birth, so that it might devour her child the moment he was born.

And *Revelation* (12:7-9):

Then war broke out in heaven. Michael and his angels fought against the dragon, and the dragon and his angels fought back. But he was not strong enough, and they lost their place in heaven. The great dragon was hurled down — that ancient serpent called the devil, or Satan, who leads the whole world astray. He was hurled to the earth, and his angels with him.

And in the *Book of Daniel* (14:22-7):

Now in that place there was a great dragon, which the Babylonians revered. The king said to Daniel, "You cannot deny that this is a living god; so worship him." Daniel said, "I worship the Lord my God, for he is the living God. But give me permission, O king, and I will kill the dragon without sword or club." The king said, "I give you permission."

Then Daniel took pitch, fat, and hair, and boiled them together and made cakes, which he fed to the dragon. The dragon ate them, and burst open. Then Daniel said, "See what you have been worshiping!"

When the Babylonians heard about it, they were very indignant and conspired against the king, saying, "The king has become a Jew; he has destroyed Bel, and killed the dragon, and slaughtered the priests." Going to the king, they said, "Hand Daniel over to us, or else we will kill you and your household." The king saw that they were pressing him hard, and under compulsion he handed Daniel over to them.

St Michael and the dragon.

Our tales now turn from dragons being defeated by heroes to prove their worth to saints vanquishing the satanic dragon. St George, a Roman military officer of the third century, is the most renowned English dragon slayer but he wasn't originally. This feature was added around the tenth century and printed by Caxton in *Golden Legend*:

S. George was a knight and born in Cappadocia. On a time he came in to the province of Libya, to a city which is said Silene. And by this city was a stagne or a pond like a sea, wherein was a dragon which envenomed all the country. And on a time the people were assembled for to slay him, and when they saw him they fled. And when he came nigh the city he venomed the people with his breath, and therefore the people of the city gave to him every day two sheep for to feed him, because he should do no harm to the people, and when the sheep failed there was taken a man and a sheep. Then was an ordinance made in the town that there should be taken the children and young people of them of the town by lot, and every each one as it fell, were he gentle or poor, should be delivered when the lot fell on him or her. So it happed that many of them of the town were then delivered, insomuch that the lot fell upon the king's daughter, whereof the king was sorry, and said unto the people: For the love of the gods take gold and silver and all that I have, and let me have my daughter. They said: How sir! ye have made and ordained the law, and our children be now dead, and ye would do the contrary. Your daughter shall be given, or else we shall burn you and your house.

When the king saw he might no more do, he began to weep, and said to his daughter: Now shall I never see thine espousals. Then returned he to the people and demanded eight days' respite, and they granted it to him. And when the eight days were passed they came to him and said: Thou seest that the city perisheth: Then did the king do array his daughter like as she should be wedded, and embraced her, kissed her and gave her his benediction, and after, led her to the place where the dragon was.

When she was there S. George passed by, and when he saw the lady he demanded the lady what she made there and she said: Go ye your way fair young man, that ye perish not also. Then said he: Tell to me what have ye and why weep ye, and doubt ye of nothing. When she saw that he would know, she said to him how she was delivered to the dragon. Then said S. George: Fair daughter, doubt ye no thing hereof for I shall help thee in the name of Jesu Christ. She said: For God's sake, good knight, go your way, and abide not with me, for ye may not deliver me. Thus as they spake together the dragon appeared and came running to them, and S. George was upon his horse, and drew out his sword and garnished him with the sign of the cross, and rode hardily against the dragon which came towards him, and smote him with his spear and hurt him sore and threw him to the ground. And after said to the maid: Deliver to me your girdle, and bind it about the neck of the dragon and be not afeard. When she had done so the dragon followed her as it had been a meek beast and debonair. Then she led him into the city, and the people fled by mountains and valleys, and said: Alas! alas! we shall be all dead. Then S. George said to them: Ne doubt ye no thing, without more, believe ye in God, Jesu Christ, and do ye to be baptized and I shall slay the dragon. Then the king was baptized and all his people, and S. George slew the dragon and smote off his head, and commanded that he should be thrown in the fields, and they took four carts with oxen that drew him out of the city.

Then were there well fifteen thousand men baptized, without women and children, and the king did do make a church there of our Lady and of S. George, in the which yet sourdeth a fountain of living water, which healeth sick people that drink thereof. After this the king offered to S. George as much money as there might be numbered, but he refused all and commanded that it should be given to poor people for God's sake; and enjoined the king four things, that is, that he should have charge of the churches, and that he should honour the priests and hear their service diligently, and that he should have pity on the poor people, and after, kissed the king and departed.

Some saints were not dragon slayers but defeated them through prayer, the cross or blessed water. Saint Marcellus of Paris battled with a dragon who strangely was living in the tomb of an adulterous

St George and the dragon.

woman. Venatius Fortunatus who wrote the *Life of Bishop Marcellus of Paris* hinted that the dragon had lured the woman to sin — like the snake in the garden of Eden — and was now feasting on her body and terrorising the citizens of Paris. Saint Marcellus went to the tomb and when he saw the dragon approaching began to pray. The dragon was stopped in his tracks and Marcellus struck it three times on the head with his crozier before putting his handkerchief on its neck and dragging it before the crowd. There he told it to either go and live in the desert or plunge itself into the sea and off it went, never to be seen again, subtly chastised.

Saint Martha's story is also told in the *Golden Legend* (or Readings of the Saints), a collection of hagiographies by Jacobus de Voragine, popular in the Middle Ages:

> At that time, in the forest along the Rhone between Aries and Avignon, there was a dragon that was half animal and half fish, larger than an ox, longer than a horse, with teeth as sharp as horns and a pair of bucklers on either side of his body. This beast lurked in the river, killing all those who tried to sail by and sinking their vessels … The people asked Martha for help, and she went after the dragon. She found him in the forest in the act of devouring a man, sprinkled him with blessed water, and had a cross held up in front of him. The brute was subdued at once and stood still like a sheep while Martha tied him up with her girdle, and the people killed him then and there with stones and lances.

Saint Margaret of Antioch was often called on by women in childbirth especially those experiencing a difficult labour. She swore to help women in delivery as she was safely delivered from the belly of a dragon. When she was in prison for her beliefs she prayed to God to reveal her enemy. A great dragon appeared and swallowed her whole. But she managed to make the sign of the cross whilst in is belly and it burst open freeing her.

There was also an Order of the Dragon founded in 1408 by Sigismund of Luxembourg, who became Holy Roman Emperor. Similar to crusading knights, it aimed to fight the enemies of Christianity and to:

> … crush the pernicious deeds of the same perfidious Enemy, and of the followers of the ancient Dragon, and

St Margaret and the dragon.

(as one would expect) of the pagan knights, schismatics, and other nations of the Orthodox faith, and those envious of the Cross of Christ, and of our kingdoms, and of his holy and saving religion of faith, under the banner of the triumphant Cross of Christ...

Their insignia was a dragon that symbolised the enemy:

… incurved into the form of a circle, its tail winding around its neck, divided through the middle of its back along its length from the top of its head right to the tip of its tail, with blood [forming] a red cross flowing out into the interior of the cleft by a white crack, untouched by blood, just as and in the same way that those who fight under the banner of the glorious martyr St George are accustomed to bear a red cross on a white field...

As can be imagined, dragons were also depicted in medieval art as foes to be vanquished but medieval bestiaries have some stunning images of all different types of dragons as they were imagined. The oldest image of a modern European dragon as we might think of it appears in the medieval manuscript MS Harley 3244 from around AD 1260 — a soaring red dragon with two sets of wings, breathing fire. Other depictions include dragons breathing fire at or wrapping themselves around elephants, some are twin-headed, others have elaborate curly tails, or lounge under trees reaching up to snag a tasty bird for a snack or surprising naked humans. And of course they also turned up in medieval literature.

Chapter 7

The Medieval Dragon in Folklore and Literature

The Western dragon as we know it today really developed during the Middle Ages. Now it was the fate of the dragon to be vanquished in a feat of arms, a test of strength or to win the hand of a fair maiden.

Beowulf, an Old English epic poem, tells us of the earliest dragon in medieval English literature. The tale of Beowulf has been told many times but usually features his fight with Grendel, a super strength being that isn't specifically identified but could be a giant or some other form of monster. Later in the poem, Beowulf encounters a dragon many years after defeating Grendel. He has ruled the land of the Geats (or Goths), a large North Germanic tribe, for more than fifty years before this dragon attacks:

> Then Beowulf came as king this broad
> realm to wield; and he ruled it well
> fifty winters, a wise old prince,
> warding his land, until One began
> in the dark of night, a Dragon, to rage.
> In the grave on the hill a hoard it guarded,
> in the stone-barrow steep. A strait path reached it,
> unknown to mortals. Some man, however,
> came by chance that cave within
> to the heathen hoard. In hand he took
> a golden goblet, nor gave he it back,
> stole with it away, while the watcher slept,
> by thievish wiles: for the warden's wrath
> prince and people must pay betimes!

This gives us the most enduring depiction of a dragon guarding his golden hoard and also one that breathes fire. As in the course of their battle, the dragon uses it in his defence:

> The bold king again
> had mind of his glory: with might his glaive
> was driven into the dragon's head, —
> blow nerved by hate. But Naegling was shivered,
> broken in battle was Beowulf's sword,
> old and gray. 'Twas granted him not
> that ever the edge of iron at all
> could help him at strife: too strong was his hand,
> so the tale is told, and he tried too far
> with strength of stroke all swords he wielded,
> though sturdy their steel: they steaded him nought.
> Then for the third time thought on its feud
> that folk-destroyer, fire-dread dragon,
> and rushed on the hero, where room allowed,
> battle-grim, burning; its bitter teeth
> closed on his neck, and covered him
> with waves of blood from his breast that welled.

Medieval dragons became the ultimate monster for heroes to defeat in ballads, romances, allegories and moral tales. In them, a hero can only prove his worth if the dragon is slain. One such story, *Bevis of Hampton* (c.1300), is a Middle English romance. It is the tale of a young boy whose mother plotted to kill his father. Guy of Southampton had married the daughter of the king of Scotland. She asked an old suitor, Doon, the emperor of Almaine (Germany) to murder her husband after which she married the emperor but Bevis threatened his mother with vengeance and beat his stepfather. She tried to kill him in return but he was saved and sold to pirates eventually reaching the court of King Hermin. His adventures are recounted, including his love

Beowulf face to face with the fire-breathing dragon.

for his beloved Josiane, King Hermin's daughter. And of course he comes across a dragon:

> Its ears were rough and long, its face hard and strong.
> Eight tusks stood out from its mouth, the least was
> Seventeen inches round. The hair and the throat under
> The chin were both loathsome and grim. It was maned
> Like a horse and carried its head with great pride.
> Between the shoulder and the tail it was undoubtedly
> Four and twenty foot. The tail was of great strength,
> sixteen feet long it was. Its body was like a wine barrel.
> When the bright sun shone its wings shone like glass.
> Its sides were hard as brass, its breast was hard as
> stone. There never was a fouler thing.

The defeat of the dragon is the ultimate test of prowess and skill as in *Sir Eglamour of Artois*, a romantic poem written around 1350. To win Cristabel, the love of his life, and her father's consent, Eglamour is set three tasks: to kill the giant Arrok; to kill a boar that is terrorising Sydon; and to slay a dragon in Rome. *Sir Degare* is another Middle English romance of around 1,100 verse lines where Degare is knighted for slaying a dragon during a quest to find his mother, whom he nearly marries! Dragons, knights, romance and adventure were some of the most loved tales of this historic period.

Guy of Warwick, or Gui de Warewic, was a bit of a legendary hero in English and French romances that were popular from the thirteenth century. He had, of course, to find a dragon and defeat it, as all good heroes should:

Guy, having given them his hearty thanks for all the undeserved honours paid him, straight hoisted sail, and, having a fair wind, in four day's time arrived on English ground; the noise of which soon reached King Athelstan, who then at York his royal palace kept: thither, being commanded by the king, he forthwith went to pay his duty and allegiance to him. The king received them (for Heraud was

Right: A dragon fresco found in a Spanish monastery. (The Metropolitan Museum of Art: The Cloisters Collection, 1931, public domain)

Below: A serpent, a winged serpent and a dragon. Woodcut after C. Gessner. (Wellcome Collection, public domain)

Sic obit, extento qui sydera respicit arcu,
Securus fati quod iacet ante pedes. Alciatus.
Hinc simile est epigramma Græcum Antipatri Sidonij de Alcimene aucupe, qui cùm arcu
& funda peteret aues in altum speculatus, ictus à Dipsade interijt, quem sic loquentem facit,

Καί μιε τίς ἐτήτεισα παρα σφυρα διψαςἔχιδνα
Σαρκὶ τὸτ ὀκγενύων πικρὸν ἐνεῖσα χόλον   30
Η ἐλίω χνέφοειν ἰδ᾽ ὡς τὰ κατ᾽ αἰθίερα λιύασων,
Τὴν ποσὶν ἐκ ἐσδαλευ πῆμα κυλινδὁμθρον.

DE DRACONE.

40

50

Jason being vomited from the dragon of Colchis's mouth after it had received a drug from Athena. (Wellcome Collection, public domain)

Barham Gur kills the dragon that had killed his youth. (Wellcome Collection, 4.0 International (CC BY 4.0))

Above left: *The Furious Dragon*! (Smithsonian American Art Museum: Gift of Hyde Gillette in memory of Mabel Hyde Gillette and Edwin Fraser Gillette, public domain)

Above right: Chariot shaft fitting in the form of a dragon head, c.4th century BCE, Late Eastern Zhou dynasty. (Smithsonian American Art Museum, public domain)

Saint Michael and the Dragon, Spanish, c.1405. (The Metropolitan Museum of Art, public domain)

William De
Morgan:
Blue Dragon.
(Wikimedia
Commons,
public domain)

Velvet Textile for
a Dragon Robe.
(The Metropolitan
Museum of Art,
public domain)

*Bell and
the Dragon*
by Thomas
Rowlandson
(1757–1827).
(Metropolitan
Museum of
Art: The Elisha
Whittelsey
Collection,
public domain)

Alexander fighting a crowned dragon. (National Library of Wales, public domain)

Ryugu Tamatori Hime no su Recovering the Stolen Jewel from the Palace of the Dragon King by Utagawa Kuniyoshi. (The Metropolitan Museum of Art, public domain)

Above left: Frontispiece to chapter 12 of 1905 edition of *The Face in the Pool* by J. Allen St John. (Wikimedia Commons, public domain)

Above right: Dragon painting by Gustave Moreau. (Wikimedia Commons, public domain)

Left: *Umar Defeats a Dragon* by Daswanth. (Wikimedia Commons, public domain)

with Guy wherever he went) with so much joy and goodness that nothing could be more; welcoming them with such kind of words as these:

'Welcome to me, renowned martial man, my princely love upon you I bestow; I in your fortunate success rejoice, for fame has loudly told us all your story. Guy, thou hast laid a heavy hand, I hear, on Pagan infidels, and with thy sword hast sent them home to the dark vaults where unbelievers dwell. Devouring beasts thou also hast destroyed, which have the terror been of human creatures: yet, worthy man, I think thou never didst slay, of all those monster terrible and wild, a creature that is more cruel that there is one that at this day destroys whatever he meets, no farther off than is Northumberland, which is a dreadful dragon that haunts there. I speak not this to animate thee on, and hazard thy life at setting foot on shore; for divers have endeavoured to destroy this wicked beast, and perished in the attempt. No, guy, I speak only to show thy happiness, which has exceeded that of other men, by freeing of them from their fears and dangers.'

'Dear lord,' said Guy, 'as I am an English knight, faithful to God, and loyal to my king, I am resolved to go and see this dragon, and try whether my sword cannot work upon him; for I already have a dragon killed, with whom a lion first I found engaged, and whom he had also like to have overcome; but heaven my arm so strengthened that I soon overcame his power, and so I will do this.' Then, taking his humble leave, away he rides unto Northumberland to find the dragon, having a dozen knights to be his guides, who brought him where the dragon kept his den, feasting himself with nought but human flesh: 'Now it is enough,' said Guy, 'do you stand off, and give me leave to find this hydra's head. He that has fed so much on human flesh shall never more devour a man again; but, gentlemen, if here you please to stay, you of our battle may spectator be.'

Then going to the cave, the dragon espied him, and forth he starts with lofty speckled breast, of form most dreadful; which when Guy beheld, into its rest he forthwith puts his lance, then spurs his horse, and to the dragon makes, encountering each the other with such fury as shook the very ground under them. Then Guy recoils and turns about his horse, and comes upon him with redoubled might: the dragon meets him with resistless force, and, like a reed, bit his strong lance in two. 'Nay, then,' said Guy, 'if you are good at biting, I have a tool to pick your teeth withal;' and drew his never failing flaming sword, and on him fell, with furious blows so fierce that many wide and bloody wounds he made. At which the dragon yawned, like hell's wide mouth, roaring aloud with a most hideous noise, and with his claws he rent and tore the ground. Impatient of the smart he underwent, he with his wings would raise his body up, but Guy, with a bold stroke, so cooled his courage that to distend his wings he wanted strength; and, with a few strokes more, Guy brought him down upon the ground, all wallowing in his blood, and from his mouth a fiery flake proceeded whilst Guy with all his might was severing his monstrous head from his more monstrous body; which when he had done,

'Now, bloody fiend,' said he, 'thou hast thy deserved recompence for all the human blood which thou hast shed. And now upon this broken piece of spear unto the king I will bear thy monstrous head, which will by him, I am sure, be well accepted.'

The joyful knights then went and took a view of that same fearful creature without fear, which was indeed of strange and ugly hue; all wondering how it was possible to escape those teeth and claws so dreadful, sharp, and long. And when they had fixed the head upon a spear, and took measure of the body's length unto the king, who had removed his court from York to Lincoln, they repair with speed where he with some impatience waited their return; who in his arms embraced the warlike Guy, congratulating him on his victory: then, looking on the dragon's fearful head, 'Heaven shield,' said he, 'and save me from all harm! Why, here is a face may well outface the devil. What staring eyes of burning glass be these, that might, alive, two flaming beacons seem! What scales of harness arm the crooked nose! And teeth more strong and sharp than those of steel! And also that gaping mouth and forked tongue may, even dead, make all the living fear, but more rejoice that thou hast overcome it. Victorious knight, thy actions we admire, and place thee highly in our royal favour: throughout the spacious orb thy fame shall spread more lofty than the primum mobile. To the succeeding age of the world thy victories shall be transmitted down; for I will have the monster's picture drawn on cloth of Arras, curiously wrought, which I in Warwick Castle will have placed, there to remain, and tell to after ages that worthy Guy, a man of matchless strength, and equal courage, destroyed a dragon thirty foot in length. And on this castle wall we will place his head, there to remain till length of time consume it. And, nobles all, make a triumphant festival, and give our knight the honour that he merits'.

We all know the tales of King Arthur and Merlin but an earlier story found in the *Historia Brittonum* (History of the Britons) tells of an unknown boy plucked from obscurity whose tales would later grow and grow in the retelling. King Vortigern wanted to build his castle at Dinas Emrys but every night, after his workers had downed

Guy of Warwick defeating a dragon.

tools, the said tools would go missing and the walls would crumble back down. Vortigern consulted his advisers who told him to find a boy with an otherworldly father and shed his blood as sacrifice. Vortigern did find such a boy, Myrddin Emrys, who would later be referred to as Merlin, who told him there were two dragons sleeping next to a lake in the mountain they were building on. His workers dug down and their digging awoke the dragons, one red (for the people of Vortigern) and one white (for the Saxons). The boy's life was saved and Vortigern was able to build his castle as the two dragons rose to the air and fought until the white dragon was vanquished. The red dragon of Wales was able to go back to sleep under the mountain.

But Merlin would go on to live through Vortigern's reign and was there when Aurelius Ambrosius became king. He would be succeeded by his brother, Uther, who going into battle against Vortigern's son, saw a comet in the shape of a dragon flying across the sky. Merlin predicted Aurelius' death and that Uther would become a great king, then to be known as Uther Pendragon and father to Arthur Pendragon. His stories would be written later but prior to 1210, Arthurian romance came mainly in the form of poetry and thereafter prose. Before being collated into tomes like Malory's *Morte d'Arthur*, one collection of prose romances was the *Vulgate Cycle* (also known as the Lancelot-Grail Cycle), which included the quest for the Holy Grail but with much more background and further tales of dragon slaying.

The knight Sir Lancelot, famous for his illicit love affair with Guinevere (Arthur's queen) slays a dragon but it leads to him being tricked. Lancelot, ever the consummate knight, goes to the aid of the people of Corbenic who are being terrorised by a dragon who sleeps in a tombstone. The inscription on the stone says that only the greatest knight in the world could lift it and that he would go on to beget a great lion from the daughter of the king of the Land Beyond. Lancelot takes no notice and lifts the lid. A huge dragon arises from its slumber and rains fire down on him. Protected by his shield, Lancelot runs his lance through its chest and then with his sword, he beheads it. King Pelles, the Grail King, (he of the Land Beyond) invites him to

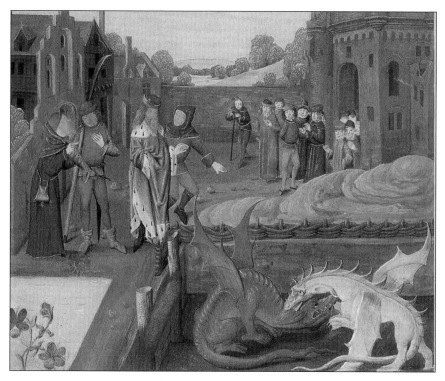

Vortigern and the dragons.

his castle to celebrate the dragon's demise, where Lancelot is tricked into sleeping with the king's daughter, Elaine. She conceives a child, Galahad, a knight who would go on to have his own adventures.

Sir Gawain, in the *Romance of Walewein*, sees a magical chessboard that then flies out of his reach so he decides to pursue it to give it as a gift to the king. On his journey he comes across a dragon and her four babies. In one of the saddest tales if you are a dragon-lover, he stabs two of the babies with his sword, rips one apart by its jaws and after Gringolet (his war horse) breaks one of the baby's leg with a stomp, he stabs that too. Their mother shares the same fate with a stab to the heart after being wedged in a cave with a lance stuck in her side. Dragons appear in several of the Arthurian tales and unfortunately never have a happy fate.

Another medieval chivalric romance from the twelfth century is that of Tristan and Isolde, the tragic love story of a Cornish knight and an Irish princess. Tristan must ask her parents to give her hand in marriage to his uncle, King Mark of Cornwall, but must slay a dragon that is terrorising the Emerald Isle before he is given permission to take her to England. Her current betrothed pretends it is he who has killed the dragon but Tristan shows her parents the dragon's tongue and he is then allowed to accompany Isolde from Ireland to marry his uncle. On the journey, Tristan and Isolde drink a love potion meant for Isolde and King Mark that sparks their forbidden desire for each other.

Outside of Arthurian-based legend, stories of Gerolde the dragon hunter were akin to St George slaying the dragon except he went for it on a large scale! Gerolde was the rockstar of his days. He and his band of men scoured the land seeking out dragons to kill. He wore super shiny armour so that the sun's rays would glint off it and blind the dragons, so he could easily kill them with his lance. But he got a

An illumination from the 14th-century Italian copy of the *Queste del Saint Graal*. (BNF Français 343: Queste del Saint Graal/ Tristan de Léonois.)

bit cocky with all the adoration and gifts he received. Women gave him their favours (little ribbons to tie on his armour) but he had so many he decided to make a jacket of them. Looking incredibly fly, he didn't stop to consider the jacket actually covered up his armour, dulling its shine so the dragons were no longer blinded and did what all good dragons do — they breathed fire and Gerolde ended up a pile of ash.

A popular book of the times was *Travels of Sir John Mandeville*, published as a travel memoir of an Englishman named Sir John Mandeville (although fictional). It tells of his journey across the Islamic world to India and China and in chapter IV, he recounts the tale of a dragon lady:

And some men say, that in the isle of Lango is yet the daughter of Ypocras, in form and likeness of a great dragon, that is a hundred fathom of length, as men say, for I have not seen her. And they of the isles call her Lady of the Land. And she lieth in an old castle, in a cave, and sheweth twice or thrice in the year, and she doth no harm to no man, but if men do her harm. And she was thus changed and transformed, from a fair damosel, into likeness of a dragon, by a goddess that was clept Diana. And men say, that she shall so endure in that form of a dragon, unto [the] time that a knight come, that is so hardy, that dare come to her and kiss her on the mouth; and then shall she turn again to her own kind, and be a woman again, but after that she shall not live long.

And it is not long sithen, that a knight of Rhodes, that was hardy and doughty in arms, said that he would kiss her. And when he was upon his courser, and went to the castle, and entered into the cave, the dragon lift up her head against him. And when the knight saw her in that form so hideous and so horrible he fled away. And the dragon bare the knight upon a rock, maugre his head; and from that rock, she cast him into the sea. And so was lost both horse and man.

And also a young man, that wist not of the dragon, went out of a ship, and went through the isle till that he came to the castle, and came into the cave, and went so long, till that he found a chamber; and there he saw a damosel that combed her head and looked in a mirror; and she had much treasure about her. And he trowed that she had been a common woman, that dwelled there to receive men to folly. And he abode, till the damosel saw the shadow of him in the mirror. And she turned her toward him, and asked him what he would? And he said, he would be her leman or paramour. And she asked him, if that he were a knight? And he said, nay. And then she said, that he might not be her leman; but she bade him go again unto his fellows, and make him knight, and come again upon the morrow, and she should come out of the cave before him, and then come and kiss her on the mouth and have no dread, — for I shall do thee no manner of harm, albeit that thou see me in likeness of a dragon; for though thou see me hideous and horrible to look on, I do thee to wit that it is made by enchantment; for without doubt, I am none other than thou seest now, a woman, and therefore dread thee nought. And if thou kiss me, thou shalt have all this treasure, and be my lord, and lord also of all the isle.

And he departed from her and went to his fellows to ship, and let make him knight and came again upon the morrow for to kiss this damosel. And when he saw her come out of the cave in form of a dragon, so hideous and so horrible, he had so great dread, that he fled again to the ship, and she followed him. And when she saw that he turned not again, she began to cry, as a thing that had much sorrow; and then she turned again into her cave. And anon the knight died. And sithen hitherward might no knight see her, but that he died anon. But when a knight cometh, that is so hardy to kiss her, he shall not die; but he shall turn the damosel into her right form and kindly shape, and he shall be lord of all the countries and isles abovesaid.

In Medieval folklore, if dragon urine dropped from the sky it could burn you, a dragon's breath could poison wells and streams and of course only true heroes could defeat a dragon. Dragon slayers, heroes and maidens became a familiar trope in literature and folklore and its where they would stay. The belief in dragons as natural beasts was dying out. The Swedish naturalist, Carolus Linnaeus, published his *Regnum Animale*, the first edition of which included dragons in a list

Dragon illustration in a 13th century manuscript.

entitled 'paradoxa', meaning marvellous or strange, but they were still listed as an animal. But by 1740 and the second edition, they had been taken out — no longer a creature to be considered in the world of natural science.

There were still some dissenters like Charles Gould who wrote in his 1886 book, *Mythical Monsters*:

> For me the major part of these creatures are not chimaeras but objects of rational study. The dragon, in place of

being a creature evolved out of the imagination of Aryan man by the contemplation of lightning flashing through the caverns which he tenanted, as is held by some mythologists, is an animal which once lived and dragged its ponderous coils, and perhaps flew; which devastated herds, and on occasions swallowed their shepherd; which, establishing its lair in some cavern overlooking the fertile plain, spread terror and destruction around, and, protected from assault by dread or superstitious feeling, may even have been subsidised by the terror-stricken peasantry, who, failing the power to destroy it, may have preferred tethering offerings of cattle adjacent to its cavern to having it come down to seek supplies from amongst their midst.

But scientific progress heralded the death of the dragon as a recognised species and was about to relegate them to the realm of story.

Chapter 8

Dragon Tales from the West

There are many, many tales of dragons from all over the world but in the next two chapters we will focus on stories from the West and tales from the East.

John Trundle, wrote this humorous account of a dragon terrorising Sussex in 1614 with the fabulous title *The Dragon, True and Wonderfull; a discourse relating a strange and monstrous serpent, or dragon, lately discovered and yet living to the great annoyance and divers slaughters both men and cattel, by his strong and violent poison*:

In Sussex, there is a pretty market-town called Horsham, near unto it a forest, called St. Leonards forest, and there, in a vast and unfrequented place, heathy, vaulty, full of unwholesome shades, and overgrown hollows, where this serpent is thought to be bred; but, wheresoever bred, certain and too true it is that there it yet lives. Within three or four miles compass are its usual haunts, oftentimes at a place called Faygate, and it hath been seen within half a mile of Horsham, a wonder, no doubt, most terrible and noisome to the inhabitants thereabouts. There is always in his track or path left a glutinous and slimy matter (as by a small similitude we may perceive in a snail's) which is very corrupt and offensive to the scent, insomuch that they perceive the air to be putrified withal, which must needs be very dangerous. For though the corruption of it cannot strike the outward part of a man, unless heated into his blood, yet by receiving it in at any of our breathing organs (the mouth or nose) it is by authority of all authors, writing in that kind, mortal and deadly, as one thus saith:

Noxia serpentum est admixto sanguine pestis. LUCAN.

to marry her. So he sent word home that he was going to bring a new queen to Bamborough Castle.Princess Margaret was not very glad to hear of her mother's place being taken, but she did not repine, but did her father's bidding, and at the appointed day came down to the castle gate with the keys all ready to hand over to her stepmother. Soon the procession drew near, and the new queen came towards Princess Margaret, who bowed low and handed her the keys of the castle. She stood there with blushing cheeks and eyes on ground, and said: 'O welcome, father dear, to your halls and bowers, and welcome to you, my new mother, for all that's here is yours,' and again she offered the keys. One of the king's knights who had escorted the new queen cried out in admiration: 'Surely this Northern princess is the loveliest of her kind.' At that the new queen flushed up and cried out: 'At least your courtesy might have excepted me,' and then she muttered below her breath: 'I'll soon put an end to her beauty.'That same night the queen, who was a noted witch, stole down to a lonely dungeon wherein she did her magic and with spells three times three, and with passes nine times nine she cast Princess Margaret under her spell. And this was her spell:

> I weird ye to be a Laidly Worm,
> And borrowed shall ye never be,
> Until Childe Wynd, the King's own son
> Come to the Heugh and thrice kiss thee;
> Until the world comes to an end,
> Borrowed shall ye never be.

So Lady Margaret went to bed a beauteous maiden, and rose up a Laidly Worm. And when her maidens came in to dress her in the morning they found coiled up on the bed a dreadful dragon, which uncoiled itself and came towards them. But they ran away shrieking, and the Laidly Worm crawled and crept, and crept and crawled till it reached the Heugh or rock of the Spindleston round which it coiled itself, and lay there basking with its terrible snout in the air.

Soon the country round about had reason to know of the Laidly Worm of Spindleston Heugh. For hunger drove the monster out from its cave and it used to devour everything it could come across. So at last they went to a mighty warlock and asked him what they should do. Then he consulted his works and familiar, and told them: 'The Laidly Worm is really the Princess Margaret and it is hunger that drives her forth to do such deeds. Put aside for her seven kine, and each day as the sun goes down, carry every drop of milk they yield to the stone trough at the foot of the Heugh, and the Laidly Worm will trouble the country no longer. But if ye would that she be borrowed to her natural shape, and that she who bespelled her be rightly punished, send over the seas for her brother, Childe Wynd.'

All was done as the warlock advised; the Laidly Worm lived on the milk of the seven kine, and the country was troubled no longer. But when Childe Wynd heard the news, he swore a mighty oath to rescue his sister and revenge her on her cruel stepmother. And three-and-thirty of his men took the oath with him. Then they set to work and built a long ship, and its keel they made of the rowan-tree. And when all was ready, they out with their oars and pulled sheer for Bamborough Keep.

But as they got near the keep the stepmother felt by her magic power that something was being wrought against her, so she summoned her familiar imps and said: 'Childe Wynd is coming over the seas; he must never land. Raise storms, or bore the hull, but nohow must he touch the shore.' Then the imps went forth to meet Childe Wynd's ship, but when they got near they found they had no power over the ship, for its keel was made of the rowan-tree. So back they came to the queen witch, who knew not what to do. She ordered her men-at-arms to resist Childe Wynd if he should land near them, and by her spells she caused the Laidly Worm to wait by the entrance of the harbour.

As the ship came near, the Worm unfolded its coils, and, dipping into the sea, caught hold of the ship of Childe Wynd, and banged it off the shore. Three times Childe Wynd urged his men on to row bravely and strong, but each time the Laidly Worm kept it off the shore. Then Childe Wynd ordered the ship to be put about, and the witch-queen thought he had given up the attempt. But instead of that, he only rounded the next point and landed safe and sound in Buddle Creek, and then, with sword drawn and bow bent, rushed up, followed by his men, to fight the terrible Worm that had kept him from landing.

But the moment Childe Wynd had landed, the witch-queen's power over the Laidly Worm had gone, and she went back to her bower all alone, not an imp, nor a man-at-arms to help her, for she knew her hour was come. So when Childe Wynd came rushing up to the Laidly Worm it made no attempt to stop him or hurt him, but just as he was going to raise his sword to slay it, the voice of his own sister Margaret came from its jaws, saying:

'O, quit your sword, unbend your bow,
And give me kisses three;
For though I am a poisonous worm,
No harm I'll do to thee.'

Childe Wynd stayed his hand, but he did not know what to think if some witchery were not in it. Then said the Laidly Worm again:

'O, quit your sword, unbend your bow,
And give me kisses three;
If I'm not won ere set of sun,
Won never shall I be.'

Then Childe Wynd went up to the Laidly Worm and kissed it once; but no change came over it. Then Childe Wynd kissed it once more; but yet no change came over it. For a third time he kissed the loathsome thing, and with a hiss and a roar the Laidly Worm reared back and before Childe Wynd stood his sister Margaret. He wrapped his cloak about her, and then went up to the castle with her. When he reached the keep, he went off to the witch-queen's bower, and when

Childe·Wynd·thrice·kisses·the Laidly·Worm & rescues·his·Sister the·Princess·Margaret·

The Laidly Worm.

he saw her, he touched her with a twig of a rowan-tree. No sooner had he touched her than she shrivelled up and shrivelled up, till she became a huge ugly toad, with bold staring eyes and a horrible hiss.

She croaked and she hissed, and then hopped away down the castle steps, and Childe Wynd took his father's place as king, and they all lived happy afterwards.

But to this day a loathsome toad is seen at times haunting the neighbourhood of Bamborough Keep, and the wicked witch-queen is that Laidly Toad.

The Nunnington Dragon

This version of the Nunnington Dragon appeared in *Legendary Yorkshire* by Frederick Ross published in 1892.

Sir Peter got a sight of the serpent, and a formidable monster he appeared to be, more terrible than any he had previously met with; and he saw that it behoved him to make special provision for the combat. He pondered the matter over for a few days, and then mounted his steed and rode to Sheffield, where he employed certain cunning artificers to make him a complete suit of armour studded with razor blades. Although razors are alluded to by Homer, and have been used by the Chinese for unknown centuries, it is doubtful whether they were a staple manufacture on the banks of the Sheaf and the Rivelin in the sixth century. It is true that Chaucer speaks of a 'Sheffield whittle,' but this was eight centuries afterwards, and it is equally to be doubted whether Sheffield, even as a village, existed at that time; but anachronisms are of small moment in legends, and we are required to accept it as a fact, that the knight had his novel suit of armour fabricated in the valley of the Sheaf.

When it was completed, he returned with it to Ryedale, and gladly was he welcomed by the villagers, as the serpent had been committing more ravages amongst the population. He had a sword, a Damascus blade of wonderful keenness, which possessed certain magical properties, similar to those of King Arthur's famous Excaliber; and one morning, after donning his armour, he took the sword in his hand and went forth to the combat. His dog accompanied him, and it was with difficulty that he was prevented from leaping up in caressing gambols against the sharp razor blades.

The serpent had its den in the side of a wooded eminence near East Newton, by Stonegrave, which has since then gone by the name of Loschy Hill, in memory of the great fight between the Knight and the Dragon. Sir Peter, who was on foot, strode along boldly towards the hill, followed by his dog, which seemed to be perfectly aware that some exciting sport was before them, as he rushed about hither and thither, sniffing the air, as if his keen scent gave him intimation that o'anie of an unusual character was not far off, and he barked and growled, as if in defiance of the foe; whilst the villagers stood afar off, with eager countenances, to watch the progress of the combat. As the knight came nearer, he became aware of a pestiferous odour that seemed to contaminate the air; and the dog scented and sniffed, and gave vent to more prolonged growlings and louder barking, and seemed to tremble with excitement in anticipation of the coining fray.

The serpent had not yet breakfasted, and seeing the man and dog approach, darted from his den and made for the clog, with which he thought to stay his appetite as a first mouthful, but the dog was too nimble and eluded his attack, leaping upon one of the curves of its body and biting it with mad excitement; whilst the knight struck it a blow with his sword which almost cut off its head, but the wound healed up instantly, and the serpent coiled itself round his body, in order to crush the life out of him, and then devour him at its leisure. It had not, in doing so, taken into account the razor blades, which cut its body in a multitude of gashes, and caused the blood to stream down on the earth; but this was not of much consequence, as it immediately uncoiled and rolled itself on the earth, when all the wounds closed up. Foiled in this attack, the monster then began to vomit out a poisonous vapour, so horrible and overcoming that the knight seemed ready to sink under its influence, but rallying his energies, he aimed a blow which cut the serpent in two, but the severed parts joined again immediately. All this time the monster was hissing in a fearful manner, and breathing out poison, and the knight began to fear he must succumb and become its prey; but determined not to give in so long as he could continue the fight, he aimed another blow with his sword and severed a portion of the tail end, although feeling persuaded that it would become reunited as before; but his dog, evidently a sagacious animal, having witnessed the former reunion, seized it in its teeth and ran off with it to a neighbouring hill, then returned and carried away other portions as they were cut off successively. The serpent writhed with pain, but afraid, or seeing the uselessness of attacking the razor-armed man, made many attempts to seize the dog, but in vain, as he was too agile to be caught; therefore he depended more on the venom of his breath at this juncture, which he continued to pour forth, and which he knew must eventually overpower his enemy.

The dog had returned from his third or fourth journey and came up to his master, wagging his tail in seeming congratulation of the cleverness with which they were gradually accomplishing the destruction of the foe, when the serpent made a spring upon him, but at the same instant the knight's magic sword descended upon his neck and severed the head from the body, which the dog at once seized and carried off to a distance, placing it on a hill near where Nunnington Church now stands. The monster was now dead which had caused so much terror and desolation, and the villagers shouted with joy as they saw the head carried past by the dog. Meanwhile the knight stood by the remaining portion of the body as it lay prone on the earth, quivering with the remains of its vitality. He was exhausted with his exertions, but more by the poisonous exhalation which the body still gave forth, but in rapidly diminishing volume. He was recovering from its effects and was waiting awhile to gain sufficient energy to leave the scene of his triumph, when the dog returned, but apparently in a very languid condition; still, however, evincing marks of satisfaction and pleasure at the conquest he and his master had achieved. The knight stooped down to pat caressingly his faithful companion, who, in return, reached up and licked his face. Unfortunately, in carrying away the head, the seat of the venom, the dog had imbibed the poison, and in licking his master's face had imparted the virus to him, and a few minutes were sufficient to produce its fatal effects, the knight and his dog falling to the earth together, and when the villagers came up they found both dead.

And here's the tale of ***The Longwitton Dragon*** from Northumberland:

In a wood not far from the village of Longwitton are three wells which have been famous for many years. Long ago people used to travel from far and near to drink the water from the wells, for it was as sweet as wine and had great healing powers. Many a shepherd whose bones ached after the long wet winter on the hills came to drink and ease his pains, and many a sickly child found new health there. The people of Longwitton were justly proud of their wells, for there seemed to be magic in them.

One day, however, a ploughman going to quench his thirst was alarmed to find a huge dragon there. It had coiled its tail round one of the trees, and pushed its long black tongue into the well, and was lapping the water like a dog. When it heard him approach it vanished; but the ploughman knew that it had only made itself invisible, for he heard its claws in the dead leaves and felt its hot breath on his face. He fled from it in terror, and only escaped by zigzagging through the trees.

From that day no pilgrim dared visit the magic wells, for the dragon haunted them. It was a fearsome monster, with a skin as warty as a toad's and a long tail like a big lizard's. It tore up the ground with its claws, and scraped the bark from the trees as it brushed past them. But few people caught sight of it, for when anyone drew near, it made itself invisible, and nothing could be seen except the leaves trembling before its breath and the flowers being crushed beneath its feet. It did little harm, and seemed content to live alone in the wood and drink from the wells; but whenever the men of Longwitton set out to attack it, it was infuriated, and the trees shook round about it as if a whirlwind had suddenly struck the wood. It seemed to have claimed the wells and would not give them up to anyone. The wells grew overgrown and untidy, while the shepherds had to nurse their aches as best they could. But one day there came riding by Longwitton a knight in search of adventure.

'We have here a jealous dragon, sir,' said the people of Longwitton to him, 'which we would gladly be rid of, but it has the power of making itself invisible, and no man can get near enough to strike a blow at it.'

'I will overcome that difficulty,' said the knight. 'I will stay here to-night, and give battle to the dragon to-morrow.'

So the next morning he anointed his eyes with a magic ointment which he had been given on his travels, and rode to the wood. The dragon was lying sleeping near one of the wells, but when it heard the sound of the horse's hoofs in the dry leaves, its ears pricked up and the spines on its back rose. Then trusting to its invisibility, it charged.

The knight was ready. The dragon, over-careless, struck wildly with its claws, and the knight plunged his sword into its side. The dragon roared with pain, for the wound was severe, but it backed quickly until it stood defending the well, and prepared to attack again. But no matter how dreadful a wound the knight inflicted, the dragon seemed to keep its strength, and the wounds healed as quickly as they were received. For hours they fought, the dragon with its clumsy movements being no match for the nimbler man; but at last the knight, worn out and arm-weary, rode away. He was almost ashamed to confess his failure to the villagers, but he was not easily dismayed.

'I will fight the dragon again to-morrow,' he said.

But the next day, although he delivered enough blows to kill a thousand dragons, the beast was as strong at the end of the day as at the beginning, and the knight was forced to retire again.

'I will try a third time,' he said. 'This dragon must possess some other magical power which I have not noticed. To-morrow I will use my eyes more and my arm less.' So he went out the third day, and for the third time attacked the dragon. But this time, as he laid about him, he kept his eyes wide open, and at last he noticed that no matter how fiercely he drove against the dragon it would not stir from the well;

and then looking more clearly he observed that it always lay so that the tip of its tail dipped into the water.

'Ah! That is the secret,' he said. And he dismounted from his horse, and led a little into the wood. Then he approached the dragon on foot, and pierced it lightly here and there till, enraged, it roared wildly and leapt at him. Then he retreated, fighting faintly and deluding the monster into thinking that he was exhausted and beaten. Step by step he fell back until he had lured it from the well. Then suddenly leaping on to his horse he rode round the dragon, and placed himself between it and the well. The dragon perceiving how it had been tricked roared like a mad bull, and fought desperately to get back to the well. But the knight, knowing now that he had mastered it, dealt it blow on blow, and this time every wound weakened it more and more. The blood dripped from its side and burned the grass beneath it; it grew feebler and feebler, until it fell heavily and lay still.

The next day the people of Longwitton buried it. Then they tidied the wells, and sent out news that the monster was dead, and there was rejoicing that night in every cottage for twenty miles around.

Perhaps the most famous dragon fight in poetry is in Edmund Spenser's *The Fairie Queen*, one of the longest poems in English with over 36,000 lines. The first three books were first published in 1590, then republished in 1596 together with books four to six. Here Canto XI is reproduced.

CANTO XI
The knight with that old Dragon fights
two dayes incessantly;
The third him overthrowes, and gayns
most glorious victory.

I
High time now gan it wex for Una faire,
To thinke of those her captive Parents deare,
And their forwasted kingdome to repaire:

Whereto whenas they now approched neare,
With hartie wordes her knight she gan to cheare,
And in her modest manner thus bespake;
Deare knight, as deare as ever knight was deare,
That all these sorrowes suffer for my sake,
High heaven behold the tedious toyle ye for me take.

II
Now are we come unto my native soyle,
And to the place where all our perils dwell;
Here haunts that feend, and does his dayly spoyle;
Therefore henceforth be at your keeping well,
And ever ready for your foeman fell.
The sparke of noble courage now awake,
And strive your excellent selfe to excell:
That shall ye evermore renowmed make,
Above all knights on earth that batteill undertake.

III
And pointing forth, Lo yonder is (said she)
The brasen towre in which my parents deare
For dread of that huge feend emprisond be,
Whom I from far, see on the walles appeare,
Whose sight my feeble soule doth greatly cheare:
And on the top of all I do espye
The watchman wayting tydings glad to heare,
That O my parents might I happily
Unto you bring, to ease you of your misery.

IV
With that they heard a roaring hideous sound,
That all the ayre with terrour filled wide,
And seemd uneath to shake the stedfast ground.
Eftsoones that dreadful Dragon they espide,

Where stretcht he lay upon the sunny side,
Of a great hill, himselfe like a great hill.
But all so soone as he from far descride
Those glistring armes, that heaven with light did fill,
He rousd himselfe full blith, and hastned them untill.

V
Then bad the knight his Lady yede aloofe,
And to an hill her selfe withdraw aside:
From whence she might behold that battailles proof,
And eke be safe from daunger far descryde:
She him obayd, and turnd a little wyde.
Now O thou sacred muse, most learned Dame,
Faire ympe of Phœbus and his aged bride,
The Nourse of time and everlasting fame,
That warlike hands ennoblest with immortall name;

VI
O gently come into my feeble brest,
Come gently, but not with that mighty rage,
Wherewith the martiall troupes thou doest infest,
And harts of great Heroës doest enrage,
That nought their kindled courage may aswage,
Soone as thy dreadfull trompe begins to sownd,
The God of warre with his fiers equipage
Thou doest awake, sleepe never he so sownd,
All scared nations doest with horrour sterne astownd.

VII
Faire Goddesse, lay that furious fit aside,
Till I of warres and bloody Mars do sing,
And Briton fields with Sarazin bloud bedyde,
Twixt that great Faery Queene, and Paynim king,
That with their horrour heaven and earth did ring;

A worke of labour long and endlesse prayse:
But now a while let downe that haughtie string,
And to my tunes thy second tenor rayse,
That I this man of God his godly armes may blaze.

VIII
By this the dreadfull Beast drew nigh to hand,
Halfe flying, and halfe footing in his haste,
That with his largenesse measured much land,
And made wide shadow under his huge wast,
As mountaine doth the valley overcast.
Approching nigh, he reared high afore
His body monstrous, horrible, and vast,
Which to increase his wondrous greatnesse more,
Was swoln with wrath, and poyson, and with bloudy gore.

IX
And over, all with brasen scales was armd,
Like plated coate of steele, so couched neare,
That nought mote perce, ne might his corse be harmd
With dint of sword, nor push of pointed speare;
Which, as an Eagle, seeing pray appeare,
His aery plumes doth rouze, full rudely dight;
So shaked he, that horrour was to heare,
For as the clashing of an Armour bright,
Such noyse his rouzed scales did send unto the knight.

X
His flaggy wings when forth he did display,
Were like two sayles, in which the hollow wynd
Is gathered full, and worketh speedy way:
And eke the pennes, that did his pineons bynd,
Were like mayne-yards, with flying canvas lynd;

With which whenas him list the ayre to beat,
And there by force unwonted passage find,
The cloudes before him fled for terrour great,
And all the heavens stood still amazed with his threat.

XI

His huge long tayle wound up in hundred foldes,
Does overspred his long bras-scaly backe,
Whose wreathed boughts when ever he unfoldes,
And thicke entangled knots adown does slacke,
Bespotted as with shields of red and blacke,
It sweepeth all the land behind him farre,
And of three furlongs does but litle lacke;
And at the point two stings in-fixed arre,
Both deadly sharpe, that sharpest steele exceeden farre.

XII

But stings and sharpest steele did far exceed
The sharpnesse of his cruell rending clawes;
Dead was it sure, as sure as death in deed,
What ever thing does touch his ravenous pawes,
Or what within his reach he ever drawes.
But his most hideous head my toung to tell,
Does tremble: for his deepe devouring jawes
Wide gaped, like the griesly mouth of hell,
Through which into his darke abisse all ravin fell.

XIII

And that more wondrous was, in either jaw
Threeranckes of yron teeth enraunged were,
In which yet trickling blood, and gobbets raw
Of late devoured bodies did appeare,
That sight thereof bred cold congealed feare:

Which to increase, and as atonce to kill,
A cloud of smoothering smoke and sulphure seare
Out of his stinking gorge forth steemed still,
That all the ayre about with smoke and stench did fill.

XIV
His blazing eyes, like two bright shining shields,
Did burne with wrath, and sparkled living fyre:
As two broad Beacons, set in open fields,
Send forth their flames far off to every shyre,
And warning give, that enemies conspyre,
With fire and sword the region to invade;
So flam'd his eyne with rage and rancorous yre:
But farre within, as in a hollow glade,
Those glaring lampes were set, that made a dreadfull
    shade.

From Spenser's Faery Queene (1905).

XV

So dreadfully he towards him did pas,
Forelifting up aloft his speckled brest,
And often bounding on the brused gras,
As for great joyance of his newcome guest.
Eftsoones he gan advance his haughtie crest,
As chauffed Bore his bristles doth upreare,
And shoke his scales to battell ready drest;
That made the Redcrosse knight nigh quake for feare,
As bidding bold defiance to his foeman neare.

XVI

The knight gan fairely couch his steadie speare,
And fiercely ran at him with rigorous might:
The pointed steele arriving rudely theare,
His harder hide would neither perce, nor bight,
But glauncing by forth passed forward right;
Yet sore amoved with so puissaunt push,
The wrathfull beast about him turned light,
And him so rudely passing by, did brush
With his long tayle, that horse and man to ground
   did rush.

XVII

Both horse and man up lightly rose againe,
And fresh encounter towards him addrest:
But th'idle stroke yet backe recoyld in vaine,
And found no place his deadly point to rest.
Exceeding rage enflam'd the furious beast,
To be avenged of so great despight;
For never felt his imperceable brest
So wondrous force, from hand of living wight;
Yet had he prov'd the powre of many a puissant
   knight.

XVIII

Then with his waving wings displayed wyde,
Himselfe up high he lifted from the ground,
And with strong flight did forcibly divide
The yielding aire, which nigh too feeble found
Her flitting parts, and element unsound,
To beare so great a weight: he cutting way
With his broad sayles, about him soared round:
At last low stouping with unweldie sway,
Snatcht up both horse and man, to beare them quite away.

XIX

Long he them bore above the subject plaine,
So far as Ewghen bow a shaft may send,
Till struggling strong did him at last constraine
To let them downe before his flightes end:
As hagard hauke, presuming to contend
With hardie fowle, above his hable might,
His wearie pounces all in vaine doth spend,
To trusse the pray too heavy for his flight;
Which comming downe to ground, does free it selfe by fight.

XX

He so disseized of his gryping grosse,
The knight his thrillant speare again assayd
In his bras-plated body to embosse,
And three mens strength unto the stroke he layd;
Wherewith the stiffe beame quaked, as affrayd,
And glauncing from his scaly necke, did glyde
Close under his left wing, then broad displayd:
The percing steele there wrought a wound full wyde,
That with the uncouth smart the Monster lowdly cryde.

XXI

He cryde, as raging seas are wont to rore,
When wintry storme his wrathfull wreck does threat,

The roaring billowes beat the ragged shore,
As they the earth would shoulder from her seat,
And greedy gulfe does gape, as he would eat
His neighbour element in his revenge:
Then gin the blustring brethren boldly threat,
To move the world from off his steadfast henge,
And boystrous battell make, each other to avenge.

XXII

The steely head stucke fast still in his flesh,
Till with his cruell clawes he snatcht the wood,
And quite a sunder broke. Forth flowed fresh
A gushing river of blacke goarie blood,
That drowned all the land, whereon he stood;
The streame thereof would drive a water-mill:
Trebly augmented was his furious mood
With bitter sence of his deepe rooted ill,
That flames of fire he threw forth from his large nosethrill.

XXIII

His hideous tayle then hurled he about,
And therewith all enwrapt the nimble thyes
Of his froth-fomy steed, whose courage stout
Striving to loose the knot that fast him tyes,
Himselfe in streighter bandes too rash implyes,
That to the ground he is perforce constraynd
To throw his rider: who can quickly ryse
From off the earth, with durty blood distaynd,
For that reprochfull fall right fowly he disdaynd.

XXIV

And fiercely tooke his trenchand blade in hand,
With which he stroke so furious and so fell,
That nothing scemd the puissaunce could withstand:
Upon his crest the hardned yron fell,

But his more hardned crest was armd so well,
That deeper dint therein it would not make;
Yet so extremely did the buffe him quell,
That from thenceforth he shund the like to take,
But when he saw them come, he did them still forsake.

XXV

The knight was wroth to see his stroke beguyld,
And smote againe with more outrageous might;
But backe againe the sparckling steele recoyld,
And left not any marke, where it did light,
As if in Adamant rocke it had bene pight.
The beast impatient of his smarting wound,
And of so fierce and forcible despight,
Thought with his wings to stye above the ground;
But his late wounded wing unserviceable found.

XXVI

Then full of griefe and anguish vehement,
He lowdly brayd, that like was never heard,
And from his wide devouring oven sent
A flake of fire, that, flashing in his beard,
Him all amazd, and almost made affeard:
The scorching flame sore swinged all his face,
And through his armour all his body seard,
That he could not endure so cruell cace,
But thought his armes to leave, and helmet to unlace.

XXVII

Not that great Champion of the antique world,
Whom famous Poetes verse so much doth vaunt,
And hath for twelve huge labours high extold,
So many furies and sharpe fits did haunt,
When him the poysond garment did enchaunt,

From Spenser's Faery Queene (1905).

With Centaures bloud and bloudie verses charm'd;
As did this knight twelve thousand dolours daunt,
Whom fyrie steele now burnt, that earst him arm'd,
That erst him goodly arm'd, now most of all him harm'd.

XXVIII
Faint, wearie, sore, emboyled, grieved, brent
With heat, toyle, wounds, armes, smart, and inward fire,
That never man such mischiefes did torment;
Death better were, death did he oft desire,
But death will never come, when needes require.
Whom so dismayd when that his foe beheld,
He cast to suffer him no more respire,
But gan his sturdy sterne about to weld,
And him so strongly stroke, that to the ground him feld.

XXIX
It fortuned, (as faire it then befell)
Behind his backe unweeting, where he stood,
Of auncient time there was a springing well,
From which fast trickled forth a silver flood,
Full of great vertues, and for med'cine good.
Whylome, before that cursed Dragon got
That happie land, and all with innocent blood
Defyld those sacred waves, it rightly hot
The well of life, ne yet his vertues had forgot.

XXX
For unto life the dead it could restore,
And guilt of sinfull crimes cleane wash away,
Those that with sicknesse were infected sore,
It could recure, and aged long decay
Renew, as one were borne that very day.
Both Silo this, and Jordan did excell,

And th' English Bath, and eke the German Spau;
Ne can Cephise, nor Hebrus match this well:
Into the same the knight backe overthrowen, fell.

XXXI

Now gan the golden Phœbus for to steepe
His fierie face in billowes of the west,
And his faint steedes watred in Ocean deepe,
Whiles from their journall labours they did rest,
When that infernall Monster, having kest
His wearie foe into that living well,
Can high advance his broad discoloured brest,
Above his wonted pitch, with countenance fell,
And clapt his yron wings, as victor he did dwell.

XXXII

Which when his pensive Ladie saw from farre,
Great woe and sorrow did her soule assay,
As weening that the sad end of the warre,
And gan to highest God entirely pray,
That feared chance from her to turne away;
With folded hands and knees full lowly bent,
All night she watcht, ne once adowne would lay
Her daintie limbs in her sad dreriment,
But praying still did wake, and waking did lament.

XXXIII

The morrow next gan early to appeare,
That Titan rose to runne his daily race;
But early ere the morrow next gan reare
Out of the sea faire Titans deawy face,
Up rose the gentle virgin from her place,
And looked all about, if she might spy
Her loved knight to move his manly pace:

For she had great doubt of his safety,
Since late she saw him fall before his enemy.

XXXIV
At last she saw, where he upstarted brave
Out of the well, wherein he drenched lay:
As Eagle fresh out of the Ocean wave,
Where he hath left his plumes all hoary gray,
And deckt himselfe with feathers youthly gay,
Like Eyas hauke up mounts unto the skies,
His newly budded pineons to assay,
And marveiles at himselfe, still as he flies:
So new this new-borne knight to battell new did rise.

XXXV
Whom when the damned feend so fresh did spy,
No wonder if he wondred at the sight,
And doubted, whether his late enemy
It were, or other new supplied knight.
He, now to prove his late renewed might,
High brandishing his bright deaw-burning blade,
Upon his crested scalpe so sore did smite,
That to the scull a yawning wound it made;
The deadly dint his dulled senses all dismaid.

XXXVI
I wote not, whether the revenging steele
Were hardned with that holy water dew,
Wherein he fell, or sharper edge did feele,
Or his baptized hands now greater grew;
Or other secret vertue did ensew;
Else never could the force of fleshly arme,
Ne molten mettall in his blood embrew;
For till that stownd could never wight him harme,
By subtilty, nor slight, nor might, nor mighty charme.

XXXVII

The cruell wound enraged him so sore,
That loud he yelded for exceeding paine;
As hundred ramping Lyons seem'd to rore,
Whom ravenous hunger did thereto constraine:
Then gan he tosse aloft his stretched traine,
And therewith scourge the buxome aire so sore,
That to his force to yeelden it was faine;
Ne ought his sturdy strokes might stand afore,
That high trees overthrew, and rocks in peeces tore.

XXXVIII

The same advauncing high above his head,
With sharpe intended sting so rude him smot,
That to the earth him drove, as stricken dead,
Ne living wight would have him life behot:
The mortall sting his angry needle shot

From Spenser's Faery Queene (1905).

Quite through his shield, and in his shoulder seasd,
Where fast it stucke, ne would there out be got:
The griefe thereof him wondrous sore diseasd,
Ne might his ranckling paine with patience be appeasd.

XXXIX
But yet more mindfull of his honour deare,
Then of the grievous smart, which him did wring,
From loathed soile he can him lightly reare,
And strove to loose the far infixed sting:
Which when in vaine he tryde with struggeling,
Inflam'd with wrath, his raging blade he heft,
And strooke so strongly, that the knotty string
Of his huge taile he quite a sunder cleft,
Five joints thereof he hewd, and but the stump him left.

XL
Hart cannot thinke, what outrage, and what cryes,
With foule enfouldred smoake and flashing fire,
The hell-bred beast threw forth unto the skyes,
That all was covered with darkenesse dire:
Then fraught with rancour, and engorged ire,
He cast at once him to avenge for all,
And gathering up himselfe out of the mire,
With his uneven wings did fiercely fall,
Upon his sunne-bright shield, and gript it fast withall.

XLI
Much was the man encombred with his hold,
In feare to lose his weapon in his paw,
Ne wist yet, how his talaunts to unfold;
For harder was from Cerberus greedie jaw
To plucke a bone, then from his cruell claw
To reave by strength the griped gage away:

Thrise he assayd it from his foot to draw,
And thrise in vaine to draw it did assay,
It booted nought to thinke to robbe him of his pray.

XLII
Tho when he saw no power might prevaile,
His trustie sword he cald to his last aid,
Wherewith he fiercely did his foe assaile,
And double blowes about him stoutly laid,
That glauncing fire out of the yron plaid;
As sparckles from the Andvile use to fly,
When heavy hammers on the wedge are swaid;
Therewith at last he forst him to unty
One of his grasping feete, him to defend thereby.

XLIII
The other foot, fast fixed on his shield,
Whenas no strength, nor stroks mote him constraine
To loose, ne yet the warlike pledge to yield,
He smot thereat with all his might and maine,
That nought so wondrous puissaunce might sustaine;
Upon the joint the lucky steele did light,
And made such way, that hewd it quite in twaine;
The paw yett missed not his minisht might,
But hong still on the shield, as it at first was pight.

XLIV
For griefe thereof and divelish despight,
From his infernall fournace forth he threw
Huge flames, that dimmed all the heavens light,
Enrold in duskish smoke and brimstone blew:
As burning Aetna from his boyling stew
Doth belch out flames, and rockes in peeces broke,
And ragged ribs of mountains molten new,

Enwrapt in coleblacke clouds and filthy smoke,
That all the land with stench, and heaven with horror
  choke.

XLV

The heate whereof, and harmefull pestilence
So sore him noyd, that forst him to retire
A little backward for his best defence,
To save his body from the scorching fire,
Which he from hellish entrailes did expire.
It chaunst (eternall God that chaunce did guide)
As he recoiled backward, in the mire
His nigh forwearied feeble feet did slide,
And downe he fell, with dread of shame sore terrifide.

XLVI

There grew a goodly tree him faire beside,
Loaden with fruit and apples rosie red,
As they in pure vermilion had beene dide,
Whereof great vertues over all were red:
For happy life to all which thereon fed,
And life eke everlasting did befall:
Great God it planted in that blessed sted
With his Almighty hand, and did it call
The tree of life, the crime of our first fathers fall.

XLVII

In all the world like was not to be found,
Save in that soile, where all good things did grow,
And freely sprong out of the fruitfull ground,
As incorrupted Nature did them sow,
Till that dread Dragon all did overthrow.
Another like faire tree eke grew thereby,
Whereof whoso did eat, eftsoones did know

Both good and ill: O mornefull memory:
That tree through one mans fault hath doen us all to dy.

XLVIII
From that first tree forth flowd, as from a well,
A trickling streame of Balme, most soveraine
And dainty deare, which on the ground, still fell,
And overflowed all the fertile plaine,
As it had deawed bene with timely raine:
Life and long health that gratious ointment gave,
And deadly wounds could heale and reare againe
The senselesse corse appointed for the grave.
Into that same he fell: which did from death him save.

XLIX
For nigh thereto the ever damned beast
Durst not approch, for he was deadly made,
And all that life preserved did detest:
Yet he is oft adventur'd to invade.
By this the drouping day-light gan to fade,
And yield his roome to sad succeeding night,
Who with her sable mantle gan to shade
The face of earth, and wayes of living wight,
And high her burning torch set up in heaven bright.

L
When gentle Una saw the second fall
Of her deare knight, who wearie of long fight,
And faint through losse of blood, mov'd not at all,
But lay, as in a dreame of deepe delight,
Besmeard with pretious Balme, whose vertuous
    might
Did heale his wounds, and scorching heat alay,
Againe she stricken was with sore affright,

And for his safetie gan devoutly pray,
And watch the noyous night, and wait for joyous day.

LI
The joyous day gan early to appeare,
And faire Aurora from the deawy bed
Of aged Tithone gan herselfe to reare,
With rosy cheekes, for shame as blushing red;
Her golden locks for haste were loosely shed
About her eares, when Una her did marke
Clymbe to her charet, all with flowers spred;
From heaven high to chase the chearelesse darke,
With merry note her loud salutes the mounting larke.

LII
Then freshly up arose the doughtie knight,
All healed of his hurts and woundes wide,
And did himselfe to battell ready dight;
Whose early foe awaiting him beside
To have devourd, so soone as day he spyde,
When now he saw himselfe so freshly reare,
As if late fight had nought him damnifyde,
He woxe dismayd, and gan his fate to feare;
Nathlesse with wonted rage he him advaunced
    neare.

LIII
And in his first encounter, gaping wide,
He thought attonce him to have swallowd quight,
And rusht upon him with outragious pride;
Who him r'encountring fierce, as hauke in flight,
Perforce rebutted backe. The weapon bright
Taking advantage of his open jaw,
Ran through his mouth with so importune might,

That deepe emperst his darksome hollow maw,
And back retyrd, his life blood forth with all did draw.

LIV
So downe he fell, and forth his life did breath,
That vanisht into smoke and cloudes swift;
So downe he fell, that th' earth him underneath
Did grone, as feeble so great load to lift;
So downe he fell, as an huge rockie clift,
Whose false foundation waves have washt away,
With dreadfull poyse is from the mayneland rift,
And rolling downe, great Neptune doth dismay;
So downe he fell, and like an heaped mountaine lay.

LV
The knight himselfe even trembled at his fall,
So huge and horrible a masse it seem'd,
And his deare Ladie, that beheld it all,
Durst not approch for dread, which she misdeem'd;
But yet at last, whenas the direfull feend
She saw not stirre, off-shaking vaine affright,
She nigher drew, and saw that joyous end:
Then God she praysd, and thankt her faithfull knight,
That had atchieved so great a conquest by his might.

From Wales, we have the tale of ***Llud and Lefelys***:

'And the second plague,' said he, 'that is in thy dominion, behold it is a dragon. And another dragon of a foreign race is fighting with it, and striving to overcome it. And therefore does your dragon make a fearful outcry. And on this wise mayest thou come to know this. After thou hast returned home, cause the Island to be measured in its length and breadth, and in the place where thou dost find the exact central point, there cause a pit to be dug, and cause a cauldron full of the best mead that can be made to be put in the pit, with a covering of satin over the face of the cauldron. And then, in thine own person do thou remain there watching, and thou wilt see the dragons fighting in the form of terrific animals. And at length they will take the form of dragons in the air. And last of all, after wearying themselves with fierce and furious fighting, they will fall in the form of two pigs upon the covering, and they will sink in, and the covering with them, and they will draw it down to the very bottom of the cauldron. And they will drink up the whole of the mead; and after that they will sleep. Thereupon do thou immediately fold the covering around them, and bury them in a kistvaen, in the strongest place thou hast in thy dominions, and hide them in the earth. And as long as they shall bide in that strong place no plague shall come to the Island of Britain from elsewhere.'

'The cause of the third plague,' said he, 'is a mighty man of magic, who takes thy meat and thy drink and thy store. And he through illusions and charms causes every one to sleep. Therefore it is needful for thee in thy own person to watch thy food and thy provisions. And lest he should overcome thee with sleep, be there a cauldron of cold water by thy side, and when thou art oppressed with sleep, plunge into the cauldron.'

Then Lludd returned back unto his land. And immediately he summoned to him the whole of his own race and of the Coranians. And as Llevelys had taught him, he bruised the insects in water, the which he cast over them all together, and forthwith it destroyed the whole tribe of the Coranians, without hurt to any of the Britons.

And some time after this, Lludd caused the Island to be measured in its length and in its breadth. And in Oxford he found the central point, and in that place he caused the earth to be dug, and in that pit a cauldron to be set, full of the best mead that could be made, and a covering of satin over the face of it. And he himself watched that night. And while he was there, he beheld the dragons fighting. And when they were weary they fell, and came down upon the top of the satin, and drew it with them to the bottom of the cauldron. And when they had drunk the mead they slept. And in their sleep, Lludd folded the covering around them, and in the securest place he had in Snowdon, he hid them in a kistraen. Now after that this spot was called Dinas Emreis, but before that, Dinas Ffaraon. And thus the fierce outcry ceased in his dominions.

The Ceirean or Cirein

Alexander Carmichael collected a huge number of Scottish folklore, traditional and natural history tales. Amongst them is a poem about what seabeasts eat:

> Seven herrings, a salmon's fill;
> Seven salmon, a seal's fill;
> Seven seals, a large whale's fill
> Seven whales, a cirein-cròin's fill
> Seven 'cionarain-cro,' Feast of great beast of ocean

Another tale from Scotland is ***The Dragon of Loch CorrieMohr*** (Dempster, 1888: 231-2):

At Loch CorrieMohr there lived for many years a flying serpent, so terrible and wild that nobody could fish in the loch, nor come within a mile of it. At last one summer, when there was a drought and a dearth, a man said to his son, 'Let us go and fish in Loch CorrieMhor, and maybe the serpent will not heed us.' So they went; but they had not made two casts when they see her coming, swimming across the loch. The man said, 'It is time we should be out of this.' And they ran together, but the serpent outran them, and they could feel her hot breath. 'Run you, my son, for my hour is come,' said the man. So the lad fled, and his father went up into a tree, having put his cap upon his sword, and struck that into the trees root, hoping to frighten the beast. But she snuffed at the cap, and knocked down the sword, and began to wind round the tree. Then he began to shoot arrows at her; but she pulled them out with her teeth as fast as he put them into her. The last arrow had an iron head and two barbs, and was of the kind which men

Chart of terrestrial and sea monsters.

call saidh baiseh, or the death arrow, which they do not part with till the last struggle. Just as the serpent reached him, and opened her jaws to seize his feet, he shot at her open jaws with the two-barbed dart. It fastened there, and could not be pulled out. So, after a struggle, the terrible beast died, and the man got home to tell the tale. N.B.— A whole kid was taken out of the serpent at her death. — (D. M., Stack)

The Peist or Piast

In the *Táin Bó Fráech* (Cattle Raid of Fráech), one of Ireland's significant mythological tales, Fráech has to battle a péist after Ailill and Medb, the king and queen of Connacht, trick him into taking a swim in a lake inhabited by this water-dragon.

> To the bank he swam, and to Ailill was thrown, with its
> berries, the tree's torn limb:

'Ah! how heavy and fair have those clusters grown; bring
  us more,' and he turned to swim;
The mid-current was reached, but the dragon was roused
  that was guard to that rowan-tree;
And it rose from the river, on Fraech it rushed: 'Throw a
  sword from the bank!' cried he.
And no man on the bank gave the sword: they were kept
  by their fear of the queen and the king;
But her clothes from her Finnabar stripped, and she leapt
  in the river his sword to bring.
And the king from above hurled his five-barbed spear;
  the full length of a shot it sped:
At his daughter it flew, and its edge shore through two
  tresses that crowned her head:
And Fraech in his hand caught the spear as it fell, and
  backward its point he turned.
And again to the land was the spear launched well: 'twas
  a feat from the champions learned'.
Though the beast bit his side as that spear was cast, yet
  fiercely the dart was flung,
Through the purple robe of the king it passed, through the
  tunic that next him clung!
Then up sprang the youths of the court, their lord in
  danger they well might deem,
But the strong hand of Fraech had closed firm on the
  sword, and Finnabar rose from the stream.
Now with sword in his hand, at the monster's head hewed
  Fraech, on its side it sank,
And he came from the river with blade stained red, and
  the monster he dragged to the bank.
Twas then Bree's Dub-lind in the Connaught land the
  Dark Water of Fraech was named,
From that fight was it called, but the queen and the king
  went back to their dun, ashamed!

Another tale of this beast from Ireland is in ***The Three Munster Heroes and the Piast***:

A long time ago, the valleys on the south-eastern side of Mount Leinster were laid waste by a terrible animal, whose haunt was in a pool near the bridge of Thuar. It is indifferently called by the names of serpent, dragon, eel, and elephant. At last a deputation was sent to the court of the King of Munster, begging that some knight of prowess might be sent to destroy the pest; and three warriors were selected for the enterprise. One of these did not cease to boast from the beginning, that he himself alone was worthy of achieving the exploit; but, when the day of departure drew near, his heart failed him, and he insisted on renouncing the dangerous honour. However, a big, simple, quiet brother of his, who, to this time, had never done anything more remarkable than hold the plough or drive home the cows, started up from the ash-corner on hearing his brother's profession of fear, and vowed that he would devote himself for the honour of the family. So the three set forward, and arrived safely at the top of Mount Leinster, the nearest point from which they could get a glimpse of the enemy with any safety, for he had the undesirable power (as far as his neighbours were concerned) of sucking into his throat any living object that had the ill luck to come within three miles of his hold. Having taken a peep at the black pool lying far below them, and the terrible 'piast' lying in a state of coma at its side, for he was now in a stupid condition after a huge meal in which he had lately indulged, they cast lots, and our big 'omadhan' was pointed out for the first trial. Telling his comrades that if he escaped alive he would light a fire at the edge of the pool, he got himself carefully inserted into a big sack of charcoal, and, being provided with a trusty sharp skene, he had himself conveyed to the neighbouring hill of Coolgarrow to abide the awakening of the dragon. This revival taking place in the usual course, the monster turned himself round, and getting scent of flesh in the southern direction, he began to exhaust the air on that side, and the sack and its contents were soon in his gullet. Feeling the hard charcoal under his tusks, he concluded that they were bones, and swallowed his prize without any misgivings. When the champion judged that he had got well inside, he began to use his weapon underneath; and the 'piast' finding something uncomfortable going on inside, rushed into his pool with all the speed he could make, and just as he was taking the plunge, our brave and cautious Munsterman had cleared his passage, and was left high and dry on the bank. After thanking heaven devoutly, he lighted the fire, and soon the whole country was in a blaze of joy. The three warriors were granted the whole Duffrey district for their services, and the successful champion determined to raise a splendid church near the pool in memory of the thing, and to show gratitude to God for his mercy; but he was warned in a dream to follow the first living things he would meet next morning, and build wherever they would rest. At sunrise he came out, and the first objects that met his sight were a duck and drake, which flew easily before him, a mile or so, and then alighted on each side of the stream, where the church and churchyard of Templeshanbo now stand. He raised a monastery on one side, and a nunnery on the other, and I believe became prior himself. The O'Farrells, the O'Briens, and O'Kennedys boast themselves the descendants of the three Munster heroes; and for hundreds of years back men only were buried on the east side of the brook, the women being laid on the side where the nunnery was built. (Carey, 1855: 416)

A Swiss Dragon

But not all tales were fiction. Athanasius Kircher wrote in *Mundus subterraneus, quo universae denique naturae divitiae* of a time he apparently saw a real dragon:

> In 1619 as I was contemplating the serene sky by night, I saw a very bright dragon with flapping wings go from a cave in a great rock in the mount called Pilatus toward another cave, known as Flue, on the opposite side of the lake [Lucerne]. Its wings were agitated with much

celerity; its body was long as well as its tail and neck. Its head was that of a serpent with teeth, and when it was flying, sparks were coming out of it like the embers thrown by an incandescent iron when struck by smiths on an anvil. At first, I thought it was a meteor, but after observing more closely, (I saw) it was truly a dragon from the recognizable motion of the members. This I write to you, your reverence, in case you should doubt that dragons truly exist in nature.

A mythical Alpine dragon with two forelegs.

Chapter 9

Dragon Tales from the East

Whereas dragons of the West needed to be slain to prove a hero's worth or to stop them from eating humans, dragons of the East had a far more benevolent nature. The Japanese author Okakura wrote in his book *The Awakening of Japan*:

> The Eastern dragon is not the gruesome monster of medieval imagination, but the genius of strength and goodness. He is the spirit of change, therefore of life itself. Hidden in the caverns of inaccessible mountains, or coiled in the unfathomed depths of the sea, he awaits the time when he slowly rouses himself into activity. He unfolds himself in the storm clouds; he washes his mane in the blackness of the seething whirlpools. His claws are in forks of lightening; his scales begin to glisten in the bark of rain-swept pine trees. His voice is heard in the hurricane, which, scattering the withered leaves of the forest quickens a new spring.

Eastern dragon flying above turbulent waves.

There are several wonderful dragon tales contained in *The Japanese Fairybook* by Yei Theodora Ozaki, first published in 1903, as follows:

My Lord Bag of Rice

Long, long ago there lived in Japan a brave warrior known to all as Tawara Toda, or 'My Lord Bag of Rice.' His true name was Fujiwara Hidesato, and there is a very interesting story of how he came to change his name. One day he sallied forth in search of adventures, for he had the nature of a warrior and could not bear to be idle. So he buckled on his two swords, took his huge bow, much taller than himself, in his hand, and slinging his quiver on his back started out. He had not gone far when he came to the bridge of Seta-no-Karashi spanning one end of the beautiful Lake Biwa. No sooner had he set foot on the bridge than he saw lying right across his path a huge serpent-dragon. Its body was so big that it looked like the trunk of a large pine tree and it took up the whole width of the bridge. One of its huge claws rested on the parapet of one side of the bridge, while its tail lay right against the other. The monster seemed to be asleep, and as it breathed, fire and smoke came out of its nostrils.

At first Hidesato could not help feeling alarmed at the sight of this horrible reptile lying in his path, for he must either turn back or walk right over its body. He was a brave man, however, and putting aside all fear went forward dauntlessly. Crunch, crunch! he stepped now on the dragon's body, now between its coils, and without even one glance backward he went on his way.

He had only gone a few steps when he heard someone calling him from behind. On turning back he was much surprised to see that the monster dragon had entirely disappeared and in its place was a strange-looking man, who was bowing most ceremoniously to the ground. His red hair streamed over his shoulders and was surmounted by a crown in the shape of a dragon's head, and his sea-green dress was patterned with shells. Hidesato knew at once that this was no ordinary mortal and he wondered much at the strange occurrence.

Where had the dragon gone in such a short space of time? Or had it transformed itself into this man, and what did the whole thing mean? While these thoughts passed through his mind he had come up to the man on the bridge and now addressed him:

'Was it you that called me just now?'

'Yes, it was I,' answered the man; 'I have an earnest request to make to you. Do you think you can grant it to me?'

'If it is in my power to do so I will,' answered Hidesato, 'but first tell me who you are?'

'I am the Dragon King of the Lake, and my home is in these waters just under this bridge.'

'And what is it you have to ask of me?' said Hidesato.

'I want you to kill my mortal enemy the centipede, who lives on the mountain beyond,' and the Dragon King pointed to a high peak on the opposite shore of the lake. Putting aside all Fear, he went forward dauntlessly.

'I have lived now for many years in this lake and I have a large family of children and grandchildren. For some time past we have lived in terror, for a monster centipede has discovered our home, and night after night it comes and carries off one of my family. I am powerless to save them. If it goes on much longer like this, not only shall I lose all my children, but I myself must fall a victim to the monster. I am, therefore, very unhappy, and in my extremity I determined to ask the help of a human being. For many days with this intention I have waited on the bridge in the shape of the horrible serpent-dragon that you saw, in the hope that some strong brave man would come along. But all who came this way, as soon as they saw me were terrified and ran away as fast as they could. You are the first man I have found able to look at me without fear, so I knew at once that you were a man of great courage. I beg you to have pity upon me. Will you not help me and kill my enemy the centipede?'

Hidesato felt very sorry for the Dragon King on hearing his story, and readily promised to do what he could to help him. The warrior asked where the centipede lived, so that he might attack the creature at once. The Dragon King replied that its home was on the mountain Mikami, but that as it came every night at a certain hour to the palace of the lake, it would be better to wait till then. So Hidesato was conducted to the palace of the Dragon King, under the bridge. Strange to say, as he followed his host downwards the waters parted to let them pass, and his clothes did not even feel damp as he passed through the flood. Never had Hidesato seen anything so beautiful as this palace built of white marble beneath the lake. He had often heard of the Sea King's Palace at the bottom of the sea, where all the servants and retainers were salt-water fishes, but here was a magnificent building in the heart of Lake Biwa. The dainty goldfishes, red carp, and silvery trout, waited upon the Dragon King and his guest.

Hidesato was astonished at the feast that was spread for him. The dishes were crystallised lotus leaves and flowers, and the chopsticks were of the rarest ebony. As soon as they sat down, the sliding doors opened and ten lovely goldfish dancers came out, and behind them followed ten red-carp musicians with the koto and the samisen. Thus the hours flew by till midnight, and the beautiful music and dancing had banished all thoughts of the centipede. The Dragon King was about to pledge the warrior in a fresh cup of wine when the palace was suddenly shaken by a tramp, tramp! as if a mighty army had begun to march not far away.

Hidesato and his host both rose to their feet and rushed to the balcony, and the warrior saw on the opposite mountain two great balls of glowing fire coming nearer and nearer. The Dragon King stood by the warrior's side trembling with fear.

'The centipede! The centipede! Those two balls of fire are its eyes. It is coming for its prey! Now is the time to kill it.'

Hidesato looked where his host pointed, and, in the dim light of the starlit evening, behind the two balls of fire he saw the long body of an enormous centipede winding round the mountains, and the light in its hundred feet glowed like so many distant lanterns moving slowly towards the shore.

Hidesato showed not the least sign of fear. He tried to calm the Dragon King.

'Don't be afraid. I shall surely kill the centipede. Just bring me my bow and arrows.'

The Dragon King did as he was bid, and the warrior noticed that he had only three arrows left in his quiver. He took the bow, and fitting an arrow to the notch, took careful aim and let fly. The arrow hit the centipede right in the middle of its head, but instead of penetrating, it glanced off harmless and fell to the ground. Nothing daunted, Hidesato took another arrow, fitted it to the notch of the bow and let fly. Again the arrow hit the mark, it struck the centipede right in the middle of its head, only to glance off and fall to the ground. The centipede was invulnerable to weapons! When the Dragon King saw that even this brave warrior's arrows were powerless to kill the centipede, he lost heart and began to tremble with fear.

The warrior saw that he had now only one arrow left in his quiver, and if this one failed he could not kill the centipede. He looked across the waters. The huge reptile had wound its horrid body seven times round the mountain and would soon come down to the lake. Nearer and nearer gleamed the fireballs of eyes, and the light of its hundred feet began to throw reflections in the still waters of the lake.

Then suddenly the warrior remembered that he had heard that human saliva was deadly to centipedes. But this was no ordinary centipede. This was so monstrous that even to think of such a creature made one creep with horror. Hidesato determined to try his last chance. So taking his last arrow and first putting the end of it in his mouth, he fitted the notch to his bow, took careful aim once more and let fly.

This time the arrow again hit the centipede right in the middle of its head, but instead of glancing off harmlessly as before, it struck home to the creature's brain. Then with a convulsive shudder the serpentine body stopped moving, and the fiery light of its great eyes and hundred feet darkened to a dull glare like the sunset of a stormy day, and then went out in blackness. A great darkness now overspread the heavens, the thunder rolled and the lightning flashed, and the wind roared in fury, and it seemed as if the world were coming to an end. The Dragon King and his children and retainers all crouched in different parts of the palace, frightened to death, for the building was shaken to its foundations. At last the dreadful night was over. Day dawned beautiful and clear. The centipede was gone from the mountain.

Then Hidesato called to the Dragon King to come out with him on the balcony, for the centipede was dead and he had nothing more to fear. Then all the inhabitants of the palace came out with joy, and Hidesato pointed to the lake. There lay the body of the dead centipede floating on the water, which was dyed red with its blood. The gratitude of the Dragon King knew no bounds. The whole family came and bowed down before the warrior, calling him their preserver and the bravest warrior in all Japan.

Another feast was prepared, more sumptuous than the first. All kinds of fish, prepared in every imaginable way, raw, stewed, boiled and roasted, served on coral trays and crystal dishes, were put before him, and the wine was the best that Hidesato had ever tasted in his life. To add to the beauty of everything the sun shone brightly, the lake glittered like a liquid diamond, and the palace was a thousand times more beautiful by day than by night.

His host tried to persuade the warrior to stay a few days, but Hidesato insisted on going home, saying that he had now finished what he had come to do, and must return. The Dragon King and his family were all very sorry to have him leave so soon, but since he would go they begged him to accept a few small presents (so they said) in token of their gratitude to him for delivering them for ever from their horrible enemy the centipede.

As the warrior stood in the porch taking leave, a train of fish was suddenly transformed into a retinue of men, all wearing ceremonial robes and dragon's crowns on their heads to show that they were servants of the great Dragon King. The presents that they carried were as follows:

First, a large bronze bell.
Second, a bag of rice.
Third, a roll of silk.
Fourth, a cooking pot.
Fifth, a bell.

Hidesato did not want to accept all these presents, but as the Dragon King insisted, he could not well refuse. The Dragon King himself accompanied the warrior as far as the bridge, and then took leave of him with many bows and good wishes, leaving the procession of servants to accompany Hidesato to his house with the presents. The warrior's household and servants had been very much concerned when they found that he did not return the night before, but they finally concluded that he had been kept by the violent storm and had taken shelter somewhere. When the servants on the watch for his return caught sight of him they called to everyone that he was approaching and the whole household turned out to meet him, wondering much what the retinue of men, bearing presents and banners, that followed him, could mean.

As soon as the Dragon King's retainers had put down the presents they vanished, and Hidesato told all that had happened to him. The presents which he had received from the grateful Dragon King were found to be of magic power. The bell only was ordinary, and as Hidesato had no use for it he presented it to the temple near by, where it was hung up, to boom out the hour of day over the surrounding neighbourhood. The single bag of rice, however much was taken from it day after day for the meals of the knight and his whole family, never grew less — the supply in the bag was inexhaustible. The roll of silk, too, never grew shorter, though time after time long pieces were cut off to make the warrior a new suit of clothes to go to Court in at the New Year. The cooking pot was wonderful, too. No matter what was put into it, it cooked deliciously whatever was wanted without any firing — truly a very economical saucepan.

The print depicts the Buddha riding on the back of a giant sea dragon.

The fame of Hidesato's fortune spread far and wide, and as there was no need for him to spend money on rice or silk or firing, he became very rich and prosperous, and was henceforth known as My Lord Bag of Rice.

The Shinansha or the South Pointing Carriage

The compass, with its needle always pointing to the North, is quite a common thing, and no one thinks that it is remarkable now, though when it was first invented it must have been a wonder. Now long ago in China, there was a still more wonderful invention called the Shinansha. This was a kind of chariot with the figure of a man on it always pointing to the South. No matter how the chariot was placed the figure always wheeled about and pointed to the South. This curious instrument was invented by Kotei, one of the three Chinese Emperors of the mythological age. Kotei was the son of the Emperor Yuhi. Before he was born his mother had a vision which foretold that her son would be a great man.

One summer evening she went out to walk in the meadows to seek the cool breezes which blow at the end of the day and to gaze with pleasure at the star-lit heavens above her. As she looked at the North Star, strange to relate, it shot forth vivid flashes of lightning in every direction. Soon after this her son Kotei came into the world. Kotei in time grew to manhood and succeeded his father the Emperor Yuhi. His early reign was greatly troubled by the rebel Shiyu. This rebel wanted to make himself King, and many were the battles which he fought to this end. Shiyu was a wicked magician, his head was made of iron, and there was no man that could conquer him.

At last Kotei declared war against the rebel and led his army to battle, and the two armies met on a plain called Takuroku. The Emperor boldly attacked the enemy, but the magician brought down a dense fog upon the battlefield, and while the royal army were wandering about in confusion, trying to find their way, Shiyu retreated with his troops, laughing at having fooled the royal army.

No matter however strong and brave the Emperor's soldiers were, the rebel with his magic could always escape in the end.

Kotei returned to his Palace, and thought and pondered deeply as to how he should conquer the magician, for he was determined not to give up yet. After a long time he invented the Shinansha with the figure of a man always pointing South, for there were no compasses in those days. With this instrument to show him the way he need not fear the dense fogs raised up by the magician to confound his men. Kotei again declared war against Shiyu. He placed the Shinansha in front of his army and led the way to the battlefield. The battle began in earnest. The rebel was being driven backward by the royal troops when he again resorted to magic, and upon his saying some strange words in a loud voice, immediately a dense fog came down upon the battlefield.

But this time no soldier minded the fog, not one was confused. Kotei by pointing to the Shinansha could find his way and directed the army without a single mistake. He closely pursued the rebel army and drove them backward till they came to a big river. This river Kotei and his men found was swollen by the floods and impossible to cross. Shiyu by using his magic art quickly passed over with his army and shut himself up in a fortress on the opposite bank. When Kotei found his march checked he was wild with disappointment, for he had very nearly overtaken the rebel when the river stopped him. He could do nothing, for there were no boats in those days, so the Emperor ordered his tent to be pitched in the pleasantest spot that the place afforded.

One day he stepped forth from his tent and after walking about for a short time he came to a pond. Here he sat down on the bank and was lost in thought. It was autumn. The trees growing along the edge of the water were shedding their leaves, which floated hither and thither on the surface of the pond. By-and-bye, Kotei's attention was attracted to a spider on the brink of the water. The little insect was trying to get on to one of the floating leaves near by. It did so at last, and was soon floating over the water to the other side of the pond. This little incident made the clever Emperor think that he might try to make something that could carry himself and his men over the river in the same way that the leaf had carried over the spider. He set to work and persevered till he invented the first boat. When he found that it was a success he set all his men to make more, and in time there were enough boats for the whole army. Kotei now took his army across the river, and attacked Shiyu's headquarters. He gained a complete victory, and so put an end to the war which had troubled his country for so long.

This wise and good Emperor did not rest till he had secured peace and prosperity throughout his whole land. He was beloved by his subjects, who now enjoyed their happiness of peace for many long years under him. He spent a great deal of time in making inventions which would benefit his people, and he succeeded in many besides the boat and the South Pointing Shinansha. He had reigned about a hundred years when one day, as Kotei was looking upwards, the sky became suddenly red, and something came glittering like gold towards the earth. As it came nearer Kotei saw that it was a great Dragon. The Dragon approached and bowed down its head before the Emperor. The Empress and the courtiers were so frightened that they ran away screaming. But the Emperor only smiled and called to them to stop, and said:

'Do not be afraid. This is a messenger from Heaven. My time here is finished!' He then mounted the Dragon, which began to ascend towards the sky.

When the Empress and the courtiers saw this they all cried out together: 'Wait a moment! We wish to come too.' And they all ran and caught hold of the Dragon's beard and tried to mount him.

But it was impossible for so many people to ride on the Dragon. Several of them hung on to the creature's beard so that when it tried to mount the hair was pulled out and they fell to the ground. Meanwhile the Empress and a few of the courtiers were safely seated on the Dragon's back. The Dragon flew up so high in the heavens that in a short time the inmates of the Palace, who had been left behind disappointed, could see them no more.

16th-century Japanese dragon.

After some time a bow and an arrow dropped to the earth in the courtyard of the Palace. They were recognised as having belonged to the Emperor Kotei. The courtiers took them up carefully and preserved them as sacred relics in the Palace.

The Jelly Fish and the Monkey

Long, long ago, in old Japan, the Kingdom of the Sea was governed by a wonderful King. He was called Rin Jin, or the Dragon King of the Sea. His power was immense, for he was the ruler of all sea creatures both great and small, and in his keeping were the Jewels of the Ebb and Flow of the Tide. The Jewel of the Ebbing Tide when thrown into the ocean caused the sea to recede from the land, and the Jewel of the Flowing Tide made the waves to rise mountains high and to flow in upon the shore like a tidal wave.

The Palace of Rin Jin was at the bottom of the sea, and was so beautiful that no one has ever seen anything like it even in dreams. The walls were of coral, the roof of jadestone and chrysoprase, and the floors were of the finest mother-of-pearl. But the Dragon King, in spite of his wide-spreading Kingdom, his beautiful Palace and all its wonders, and his power, which none disputed throughout the whole sea, was not at all happy, for he reigned alone. At last he thought that if he married he would not only be happier, but also

152

more powerful. So he decided to take a wife. Calling all his fish retainers together, he chose several of them as ambassadors to go through the sea and seek for a young Dragon Princess who would be his bride. At last they returned to the Palace bringing with them a lovely young dragon. Her scales were of a glittering green like the wings of summer beetles, her eyes threw out glances of fire, and she was dressed in gorgeous robes. All the jewels of the sea worked in with embroidery adorned them.

The King fell in love with her at once, and the wedding ceremony was celebrated with great splendour. Every living thing in the sea, from the great whales down to the little shrimps, came in shoals to offer their congratulations to the bride and bridegroom and to wish them a long and prosperous life. Never had there been such an assemblage or such gay festivities in the Fish-World before. The train of bearers who carried the bride's possessions to her new home seemed to reach across the waves from one end of the sea to the other. Each fish carried a phosphorescent lantern and was dressed in ceremonial robes, gleaming blue and pink and silver; and the waves as they rose and fell and broke that night seemed to be rolling masses of white and green fire, for the phosphorus shone with double brilliancy in honour of the event.

Now for a time the Dragon King and his bride lived very happily. They loved each other dearly, and the bridegroom day after day took delight in showing his bride all the wonders and treasures of his coral Palace, and she was never tired of wandering with him through its vast halls and gardens. Life seemed to them both like a long summer's day. Two months passed in this happy way, and then the Dragon Queen fell ill and was obliged to stay in bed. The King was sorely troubled when he saw his precious bride so ill, and at once sent for the fish doctor to come and give her some medicine. He gave special orders to the servants to nurse her carefully and to wait upon her with diligence, but in spite of all the nurses' assiduous care and the medicine that the doctor prescribed, the young Queen showed no signs of recovery, but grew daily worse.

Then the Dragon King interviewed the doctor and blamed him for not curing the Queen. The doctor was alarmed at Rin Jin's evident displeasure, and excused his want of skill by saying that although he knew the right kind of medicine to give the invalid, it was impossible to find it in the sea.

'Do you mean to tell me that you can't get the medicine here,' asked the Dragon King.

'It is just as you say!' said the doctor.

'Tell me what it is you want for the Queen?' demanded Rin Jin.

'I want the liver of a live monkey!' answered the doctor.

'The liver of a live monkey! Of course that will be most difficult to get,' said the King.

'If we could only get that for the Queen, Her Majesty would soon recover,' said the doctor.

'Very well, that decides it; we must get it somehow or other. But where are we most likely to find a monkey?' asked the King.

Then the doctor told the Dragon King that some distance to the south there was a Monkey Island where a great many monkeys lived.

'If only you could capture one of those monkeys?' said the doctor.

'How can any of my people capture a monkey?' said the Dragon King, greatly puzzled. 'The monkeys live on dry land, while we live in the water; and out of our element we are quite powerless! I don't see what we can do!'

'That has been my difficulty too,' said the doctor.

'But amongst your innumerable servants, you surely can find one who can go on shore for that express purpose!'

'Something must be done,' said the King, and calling his chief steward he consulted him on the matter.

The chief steward thought for some time, and then, as if struck by a sudden thought, said joyfully : 'I know what we must do! There is the kurage (jelly fish). He is certainly ugly to look at, but he is proud of being able to walk on land with his four legs like a tortoise. Let us send him to the Island of Monkeys to catch one.'

The jelly fish was then summoned to the King's presence, and was told by His Majesty what was required of him. The jelly fish, on being told of the unexpected mission which was to be entrusted to him, looked very troubled and said that he had never been to the island in question, and as he had never had any experience in catching monkeys he was afraid that he would not be able to get one.

'Well,' said the chief steward, 'if you depend on your strength or dexterity you will never catch a monkey. The only way is to play a trick on one!'

'How can I play a trick on a monkey? I don't know how to do it,' said the perplexed jelly fish.

'This is what you must do,' said the wily chief steward.

'When you approach the Island of Monkeys and meet some of them, you must try to get very friendly with one. Tell him that you are a servant of the Dragon King, and invite him to come and visit you and see the Dragon King's Palace. Try and describe to him as vividly as you can the grandeur of the Palace and the wonders of the sea so as to arouse his curiosity and make him long to see it all!'

'But how am I to get the monkey here? You know monkeys don't swim!' said the reluctant jelly fish.

'You must carry him on your back. What is the use of your shell if you can't do that!' said the chief steward.

'Won't he be very heavy?' queried kurage again.

'You mustn't mind that, for you are working for the Dragon King!' replied the chief steward.

'I will do my best then,' said the jelly fish, and he swam away from the Palace and started off towards the Monkey Island. Swimming swiftly he reached his destination in a few hours, and was landed by a convenient wave upon the shore. On looking round he saw not far away a big pine-tree with drooping branches and on one of those branches was just what he was looking for — a live monkey.

'I'm in luck!' thought the jelly fish. 'Now I must flatter the creature and try to entice him to come back with me to the Palace, and my part will be done!'

So the jelly fish slowly walked towards the pine-tree. In those ancient days the jelly fish had four legs and a hard shell like a tortoise. When he got to the pine-tree he raised his voice and said :

'How do you do, Mr. Monkey? Isn't it a lovely day?'

'A very fine day,' answered the monkey from the tree.

'I have never seen you in this part of the world before. Where have you come from and what is your name?'

'My name is kurage or jelly fish. I am one of the servants of the Dragon King. I have heard so much of your beautiful island that I have come on purpose to see it,' answered the jelly fish.

'I am very glad to see you,' said the monkey.

'By-the-bye,' said the jelly fish, 'have you ever seen the Palace of the Dragon King of the Sea where I live?'

'I have often heard of it, but I have never seen it!' answered the monkey.

'Then you ought most surely to come. It is a great pity for you to go through life without seeing it. The beauty of the Palace is beyond all description — it is certainly to my mind the most lovely place in the world,' said the jelly fish.

'Is it so beautiful as all that?' asked the monkey in astonishment.

Then the jelly fish saw his chance, and went on describing to the best of his ability the beauty and grandeur of the Sea King's Palace, and the wonders of the garden with its curious trees of white, pink and red coral, and the still more curious fruits like great jewels hanging on the branches. The monkey grew more and more interested, and as he listened he came down the tree step by step so as not to lose a word of the wonderful story.

'I have got him at last!' thought the jelly fish, but aloud he said: 'Mr. Monkey, I must now go back. As you have never seen the Palace of the Dragon King, won't you avail yourself of this splendid opportunity by coming with me? I shall then be able to act as guide and show you all the sights of the sea, which will be even more wonderful to you — a land-lubber.'

'I should love to go,' said the monkey, 'but how am I to cross the water? I can't swim, as you surely know!'

'There is no difficulty about that. I can carry you on my back.'

'That will be troubling you too much,' said the monkey.

'I can do it quite easily. I am stronger than I look, so you needn't hesitate,' said the jelly fish, and taking the monkey on his back he stepped into the sea.

'Keep very still, Mr. Monkey,' said the jelly fish. 'You mustn't fall into the sea; I am responsible for your safe arrival at the King's Palace.'

'Please don't go so fast, or I am sure I shall fall off,' said the monkey.

Thus they went along, the jelly fish skimming through the waves with the monkey sitting on his back. When they were about half-way, the jelly fish, who knew very little of anatomy, began to wonder if the monkey had his liver with him or not!

'Mr. Monkey, tell me, have you such a thing as a liver with you?'

The monkey was very much surprised at this queer question, and asked what the jelly fish wanted with a liver.

'That is the most important thing of all,' said the stupid jelly fish, 'so as soon as I recollected it, I asked you if you had yours with you?'

'Why is my liver so important to you?' asked the monkey.

'Oh! you will learn the reason later,' said the jelly fish.

The monkey grew more and more curious and suspicious, and urged the jelly fish to tell him for what his liver was wanted, and ended up by appealing to his hearer's feelings by saying that he was very troubled at what he had been told.

Then the jelly fish, seeing how anxious the monkey looked, was sorry for him, and told him everything. How the Dragon Queen had fallen ill, and how the doctor had said that only the liver of a live monkey would cure her, and how the Dragon King had sent him to find one.

'Now I have done as I was told, and as soon as we arrive at the Palace the doctor will want your liver, so I feel sorry for you!' said the silly jelly fish.

The poor monkey was horrified when he learnt all this, and very angry at the trick played upon him. He trembled with fear at the thought of what was in store for him. But the monkey was a clever

Dragon King with a Tide-Ruling Jewel.

animal, and he thought it the wisest plan not to show any sign of the fear he felt, so he tried to calm himself and to think of some way by which he might escape.

'The doctor means to cut me open and then take my liver out! Why I shall die!' thought the monkey. At last a bright thought struck him, so he said quite cheerfully to the jelly fish:

'What a pity it was, Mr. Jelly Fish, that you did not speak of this before we left the island!'

'If I had told you why I wanted you to accompany me you would certainly have refused to come,' answered the jelly fish.

'You are quite mistaken,' said the monkey. 'Monkeys can very well spare a liver or two, especially when it is wanted for the Dragon Queen of the Sea. If I had only guessed of what you were in need, I should have presented you with one without waiting to be asked. I have several livers. But the greatest pity is, that as you did not speak in time, I have left all my livers hanging on the pine-tree.'

'Have you left your liver behind you?' asked the jelly fish.

'Yes,' said the cunning monkey, 'during the daytime I usually leave my liver hanging up on the branch of a tree, as it is very much in the way when I am climbing about from tree to tree. To-day, listening to your interesting conversation, I quite forgot it, and left it behind when I came off with you. If only you had spoken in time I should have remembered it, and should have brought it along with me!'

The jelly fish was very disappointed when he heard this, for he believed every word the monkey said. The monkey was of no good without a liver. Finally the jelly fish stopped and told the monkey so.

'Well,' said the monkey, 'that is soon remedied. I am really sorry to think of all your trouble; but if you will only take me back to the place where you found me, I shall soon be able to get my liver.'

The jelly fish did not at all like the idea of going all the way back to the island again; but the monkey assured him that if he would be so kind as to take him back he would get his very best liver, and bring it with him the next time. Thus persuaded, the jelly fish turned his course towards the Monkey Island once more.

No sooner had the jelly fish reached the shore than the sly monkey landed, and getting up into the pine-tree where the jelly fish had first seen him, he cut several capers amongst the branches with joy at being safe home again, and then looking down at the jelly fish said:

'So many thanks for all the trouble you have taken! Please present my compliments to the Dragon King on your return!'

The jelly fish wondered at this speech and the mocking tone in which it was uttered. Then he asked the monkey if it wasn't his intention to come with him at once after getting his liver.

The monkey replied laughingly that he couldn't afford to lose his liver; it was too precious.

'But remember your promise!' pleaded the jelly fish, now very discouraged.

'That promise was false, and anyhow it is now broken!' answered the monkey. Then he began to jeer at the jelly fish and told him that he had been deceiving him the whole time; that he had no wish to lose his life, which he certainly would have done had he gone on to the Sea King's Palace to the old doctor waiting for him, instead of persuading the jelly-fish to return under false pretences.

'Of course, I won't give you my liver, but come and get it if you can!' added the monkey mockingly from the tree.

There was nothing for the jelly fish to do now but to repent of his stupidity, and return to the Dragon King of the Sea and confess his failure, so he started sadly and slowly to swim back. The last thing he heard as he glided away, leaving the island behind him, was the monkey laughing at him.

Meanwhile the Dragon King, the doctor, the chief steward, and all the servants were waiting impatiently for the return of the jelly fish. When they caught sight of him approaching the Palace, they hailed him with delight. They began to thank him profusely for all the trouble he had taken in going to Monkey Island, and then they asked him where the monkey was.

Now the day of reckoning had come for the jelly fish. He quaked all over as he told his story. How he had brought the monkey half-way over the sea, and then had stupidly let out the secret of his commission; how the monkey had deceived him by making him believe that he had left his liver behind him.

The Dragon King's wrath was great, and he at once gave orders that the jelly fish was to be severely punished. The punishment was a horrible one. All the bones were to be drawn out from his living body, and he was to be beaten with sticks.

The poor jelly fish, humiliated and horrified beyond all words, cried out for pardon. But the Dragon King's order had to be obeyed. The servants of the Palace forthwith each brought out a stick and surrounded the jelly fish, and after pulling out his bones they beat him to a flat pulp, and then took him out beyond the Palace gates and threw him into the water. Here he was left to suffer and repent his foolish chattering, and to grow accustomed to his new state of bonelessness.

From this story it is evident that in former times the jelly fish once had a shell and bones something like a tortoise, but, ever since the Dragon King's sentence was carried out on the ancestor of the jelly fishes, his descendants have all been soft and boneless just as you see them to-day thrown up by the waves high upon the shores of Japan.

The Story of Urashima Taro, The Fisher Lad

Long, long ago in the province of Tango there lived on the shore of Japan in the little fishing village of Mizu-no-ye a young fisherman named Urashima Taro. His father had been a fisherman before him, and his skill had more than doubly descended to his son, for Urashima was the most skilful fisher in all that countryside, and could catch more bonito and tai in a day than his comrades could in a week.

But in the little fishing village, more than for being a clever fisher of the sea was he known for his kind heart. In his whole life he had never hurt anything, either great or small, and when a boy, his companions had always laughed at him, for he would never join with them in teasing animals, but always tried to keep them from this cruel sport.

One soft summer twilight he was going home at the end of a day's fishing when he came upon a group of children. They were all screaming and talking at the tops of their voices, and seemed to be in a state of great excitement about something, and on his going up to them to see what was the matter he saw that they were tormenting a tortoise. First one boy pulled it this way, then another boy pulled it that way, while a third child beat it with a stick, and the fourth hammered its shell with a stone.

Now Urashima felt very sorry for the poor tortoise and made up his mind to rescue it. He spoke to the boys:

'Look here, boys, you are treating that poor tortoise so badly that it will soon die!'

The boys, who were all of an age when children seem to delight in being cruel to animals, took no notice of Urashima's gentle reproof, but went on teasing it as before. One of the older boys answered:

'Who cares whether it lives or dies? We do not. Here, boys, go on, go on!'

And they began to treat the poor tortoise more cruelly than ever. Urashima waited a moment, turning over in his mind what would be the best way to deal with the boys. He would try to persuade them to give the tortoise up to him, so he smiled at them and said:

'I am sure you are all good, kind boys! Now won't you give me the tortoise? I should like to have it so much!'

'No, we won't give you the tortoise,' said one of the boys.

'Why should we? We caught it ourselves.'

'What you say is true,' said Urashima, 'but I do not ask you to give it to me for nothing. I will give you some money for it — in other words, the Ojisan (Uncle) will buy it off you. Won't that do for you, my boys?' He held up the money to them, strung on a piece of string through a hole in the centre of each coin. "Look, boys, you can buy anything you like with this money. You can do much more with this money than you can with that poor tortoise. See what good boys you are to listen to me.'

The boys were not bad boys at all, they were only mischievous, and as Urashima spoke they were won by his kind smile and gentle words and began 'to be of his spirit', as they say in Japan. Gradually they all came up to him, the ringleader of the little band holding out the tortoise to him.

'Very well, Ojisan, we will give you the tortoise if you will give us the money!' And Urashima took the tortoise and gave the money to the boys, who, calling to each other, scampered away and were soon out of sight.

Then Urashima stroked the tortoise's back, saying as he did so:

'Oh, you poor thing! Poor thing! — there, there! you are safe now! They say that a stork lives for a thousand years, but the tortoise for ten thousand years. You have the longest life of any creature in this world, and you were in great danger of having that precious life cut short by those cruel boys. Luckily I was passing by and saved you, and so life is still yours. Now I am going to take you back to your home, the sea, at once. Do not let yourself be caught again, for there might be no one to save you next time!'

All the time that the kind fisherman was speaking he was walking quickly to the shore and out upon the rocks; then putting the tortoise into the water he watched the animal disappear, and turned homewards himself, for he was tired and the sun had set.

The next morning Urashima went out as usual in his boat. The weather was fine and the sea and sky were both blue and soft in the tender haze of the summer morning. Urashima got into his boat and dreamily pushed out to sea, throwing his line as he did so. He soon passed the other fishing boats and left them behind him till they were lost to sight in the distance, and his boat drifted further and further out upon the blue waters. Somehow, he knew not why, he felt unusually happy that morning; and he could not help wishing that, like the tortoise he set free the day before, he had thousands of years to live instead of his own short span of human life.

He was suddenly startled from his reverie by hearing his own name called 'Urashima, Urashima!'

Clear as a bell and soft as the summer wind the name floated over the sea.

He stood up and looked in every direction, thinking that one of the other boats had overtaken him, but gaze as he might over the wide expanse of water, near or far there was no sign of a boat, so the voice could not have come from any human being.

Startled, and wondering who or what it was that had called him so clearly, he looked in all directions round about him and saw that without his knowing it a tortoise had come to the side of the boat. Urashima saw with surprise that it was the very tortoise he had rescued the day before.

'Well, Mr. Tortoise,' said Urashima, 'was it you who called my name just now?'

The tortoise nodded its head several times, and said: 'Yes, it was I. Yesterday in your honourable shadow (0 kage sama de) my life was saved, and I have come to offer you my thanks and to tell you how grateful I am for your kindness to me.'

'Indeed,' said Urashima, 'that is very polite of you. Come up into the boat. I would offer you a smoke, but as you are a tortoise doubtless you do not smoke,' and the fisherman laughed at the joke.

'He — he — he — he!' laughed the tortoise, 'sake (rice wine) is my favourite refreshment, but I do not care for tobacco.'

'Indeed,' said Urashima, 'I regret very much that I have no "sake" in my boat to offer you, but come up and dry your back in the sun — tortoises always love to do that.'

So the tortoise climbed into the boat, the fisherman helping him, and after an exchange of complimentary speeches the tortoise said: 'Have you ever seen Rin Gin, the Palace of the Dragon King of the Sea, Urashima?'

The fisherman shook his head and replied: 'No; year after year the sea has been my home, but though I have often heard of the Dragon King's realm under the sea I have never yet set eyes on that wonderful place. It must be very far away, if it exists at all!'

'Is that really so? You have never seen the Sea King's Palace? Then you have missed seeing one of the most wonderful sights in the whole universe. It is far away at the bottom of the sea, but if I take you there we shall soon reach the place. If you would like to see the Sea King's land I will be your guide.'

'I should like to go there, certainly, and you are very kind to think of taking me, but you must remember that I am only a poor mortal and have not the power of swimming like a sea creature such as you are.'

Before the fisherman could say more the tortoise stopped him, saying: 'What? You need not swim yourself. If you will ride on my back I will take you without any trouble on your part.'

'But,' said Urashima, 'how is it possible for me to ride on your small back?'

'It may seem absurd to you, but I assure you that you can do so. Try at once! Just come and get on my back, and see if it is as impossible as you think!'

As the tortoise finished speaking, Urashima looked at its shell, and strange to say he saw that the creature had suddenly grown so big that a man could easily sit on its back.

'This is strange indeed!' said Urashima; 'then, Mr. Tortoise, with your kind permission I will get on your back. Dokoisho!' He exclaimed as he jumped on.

The tortoise, with an unmoved face, as if this strange proceeding were quite an ordinary event, said: 'Now we will set out at our leisure,' and with these words he leapt into the sea with Urashima on his back. Down through the water the tortoise dived. For a long time these two strange companions rode through the sea. Urashima never grew tired, nor his clothes moist with the water. At last, far away in the distance a magnificent gate appeared, and behind the gate, the long, sloping roofs of a palace on the horizon.

'Ya,' exclaimed Urashima, 'that looks like the gate of some large palace just appearing! Mr. Tortoise, can you tell what that place is we can now see?'

'That is the great gate of the Rin Gin Palace. The large roof that you see behind the gate is the Sea King's Palace itself.'

'Then we have at last come to the realm of the Sea King and to his Palace,' said Urashima.

'Yes, indeed,' answered the tortoise, 'and don't you think we have come very quickly?' And while he was speaking the tortoise reached the side of the gate. 'And here we are, and you must please walk from here.'

The tortoise now went in front, and speaking to the gate-keeper said: 'This is Urashima Taro, from the country of Japan. I have had the honour of bringing him as a visitor to this kingdom. Please show him the way.'

Then the gatekeeper, who was a fish, at once led the way through the gate before them. The red bream, the flounder, the sole, the cuttlefish, and all the chief vassals of the Dragon King of the Sea now came out with courtly bows to welcome the stranger.

'Urashima Sama, Urashima Sama! welcome to the Sea Palace, the home of the Dragon King of the Sea. Thrice welcome are you, having come from such a distant country. And you, Mr. Tortoise, we are greatly indebted to you for all your trouble in bringing Urashima here.' Then, turning again to Urashima, they said, 'Please follow us this way,' and from here the whole band of fishes became his guides.

Urashima, being only a poor fisher lad, did not know how to behave in a palace; but, strange though it all was to him, he did not feel ashamed or embarrassed, but followed his kind guides quite calmly where they led to the inner palace. When he reached the portals a beautiful Princess with her attendant maidens came out to welcome him. She was more beautiful than any human being, and was robed in flowing garments of red and soft green like the under side of a wave, and golden threads glimmered through the folds of her gown. Her lovely black hair streamed over her shoulders in the fashion of a king's daughter many hundreds of years ago, and when she spoke her voice sounded like music over the water. Urashima was lost in wonder while he looked upon her, and he could not speak. Then he remembered that he ought to bow, but before he could make a low obeisance the Princess took him by the hand and led him to a beautiful hall, and to the seat of honour at the upper end, and bade him be seated.

'Urashima Taro, it gives me the highest pleasure to welcome you to my father's kingdom,' said the Princess.

'Yesterday you set free a tortoise, and I have sent for you to thank you for saving my life, for I was that tortoise. Now it like you shall live here for ever in the land of eternal youth, where summer never dies and where sorrow never comes, and I will be your bride if you will, and we will live together happily for ever afterwards!'

And as Urashima listened to her sweet words and gazed upon her lovely face his heart was filled with a great wonder and joy, and he answered her, wondering if it was not all a dream:

'Thank you a thousand times for your kind speech. There is nothing I could wish for more than to be permitted to stay here with you in this beautiful land, of which I have often heard, but have never seen to this day. Beyond all words, this is the most wonderful place I have ever seen.'

While he was speaking a train of fishes appeared, all dressed in ceremonial, trailing garments. One by one, silently and with stately steps, they entered the hall, bearing on coral trays delicacies of fish and seaweed, such as no one can dream of, and this wondrous feast was set before the bride and bride-groom. The bridal was celebrated with dazzling splendour, and in the Sea King's realm there was great rejoicing. As soon as the young pair had pledged themselves in the wedding cup of wine, three times three, music was played, and songs were sung, and fishes with silver scales and golden tails stepped in from the waves and danced. Urashima enjoyed himself with all his heart. Never in his whole life had he sat down to such a marvellous feast.

When the feast was over the Princess asked the bride-groom if he would like to walk through the palace and see all there was to be seen. Then the happy fisherman, following his bride, the Sea King's daughter, was shown all the wonders of that enchanted land where youth and joy go hand in hand and neither time nor age can touch them. The palace was built of coral and adorned with pearls, and the beauties and wonders of the place were so great that the tongue fails to describe them.

But, to Urashima, more wonderful than the palace was the garden that surrounded it. Here was to be seen at one time the scenery of the four different seasons; the beauties of summer and winter, spring and autumn, were displayed to the wondering visitor at once.

From The Japanese Fairy Book (1903).

First, when he looked to the east, the plum and cherry trees were seen in full bloom, the nightingales sang in the pink avenues, and butterflies flitted from flower to flower.

Looking to the south all the trees were green in the fulness of summer, and the day cicala and the night cricket chirruped loudly.

Looking to the west the autumn maples were ablaze like a sunset sky, and the chrysanthemums were in perfection.

Looking to the north the change made Urashima start, for the ground was silver white with snow, and trees and bamboos were also covered with snow and the pond was thick with ice.

And each day there were new joys and new wonders for Urashima, and so great was his happiness that he forgot everything, even the home he had left behind and his parents and his own country, and three days passed without his even thinking of all he had left behind. Then his mind came back to him and he remembered who he was, and that he did not belong to this wonderful land or the Sea King's palace, and he said to himself:

'Dear! I must not stay on here, for I have an old father and mother at home. What can have happened to them all this time? How anxious they must have been these days when I did not return as usual. I must go back at once without letting one more day pass.' And he began to prepare for the journey in great haste.

Then he went to his beautiful wife, the Princess, and bowing low before her he said: 'Indeed, I have been very happy with you for a long time, Otohime Sama' (for that was her name), 'and you have been kinder to me than any words can tell. But now I must say good-bye. I must go back to my old parents.'

Then Otohime Sama began to weep, and said softly and sadly:

'Is it not well with you here, Urashima, that you wish to leave me so soon? Where is the haste? Stay with me yet another day only!'

But Urashima had remembered his old parents, and in Japan the duty to parents is stronger than everything else, stronger even than pleasure or love, and he would not be persuaded, but answered: 'Indeed, I must go. Do not think that I wish to leave you. It is not that. I must go and see my old parents. Let me go for one day and I will come back to you.'

'Then,' said the Princess sorrowfully, 'there is nothing to be done. I will send you back to-day to your father and mother, and instead of trying to keep you with me one more day, I shall give you this as a token of our love — please take it back with you'; and she brought him a beautiful lacquer box tied about with a silken cord and tassels of red silk.

Urashima had received so much from the Princess already that he felt some compunction in taking the gift, and said: 'It does not seem right for me to take yet another gift from you after all the many favours I have received at your hands, but because it is your wish I will do so,' and then he added: 'Tell me what is this box?'

'That,' answered the Princess 'is the Tamate-Bako (Box of the Jewel Hand), and it contains something very precious. You must not open this box, whatever happens! If you open it something dreadful will happen to you! Now promise me that you will never open this box!'

And Urashima promised that he would never, never open the box whatever happened.

Then bidding good-bye to Otohime Sama he went down to the seashore, the Princess and her attendants following him, and there he found a large tortoise waiting for him.

He quickly mounted the creature's back and was carried away over the shining sea into the East. He looked back to wave his hand to Otohime Sama till at last he could see her no more, and the land of the Sea King and the roofs of the wonderful palace were lost in the far, far distance. Then, with his face turned eagerly towards his own land, he looked for the rising of the blue hills on the horizon before him.

At last the tortoise carried him into the bay he knew so well, and to the shore from whence he had set out. He stepped on to the shore and looked about him while the tortoise rode away back to the Sea King's realm.

But what is the strange fear that seizes Urashima as he stands and looks about him? Why does he gaze so fixedly at the people that pass him by, and why do they in turn stand and look at him? The shore is the same and the hills are the same, but the people that he sees walking past him have very different faces to those he had known so well before.

Wondering what it can mean he walks quickly towards his old home. Even that looks different, but a house stands on the spot, and he calls out: 'Father, I have just returned!' and he was about to enter, when he saw a strange man coming out.

'Perhaps my parents have moved while I have been away, and have gone somewhere else,' was the fisherman's thought. Somehow he began to feel strangely anxious, he could not tell why.

'Excuse me,' said he to the man who was staring at him, 'but till within the last few days I have lived in this house. My name is Urashima Taro. Where have my parents gone whom I left here?'

A very bewildered expression came over the face of the man, and, still gazing intently on Urashima's face, he said: 'What? Are you Urashima Taro?'

'Yes,' said the fisherman, 'I am Urashima Taro!'

'Ha, ha!' laughed the man, 'you must not make such jokes. It is true that once upon a time a man called Urashima Taro did live in this village, but that is a story three hundred years old. He could not possibly be alive now.'

When Urashima heard these strange words he was frightened, and said: 'Please, please, you must not joke with me, for I am greatly perplexed. I am really Urashima Taro, and I certainly have not lived three hundred years. Till four or five days ago I lived on this spot. Tell me what I want to know without more joking, please.'

But the man's face grew more and more grave, and he answered: 'You may or may not be Urashima Taro, I don't know. But the Urashima Taro of whom I have heard is a man who lived three hundred years ago. Perhaps you are his spirit come to re-visit your old home?'

'Why do you mock me?' said Urashima. 'I am no spirit! I am a living man — do you not see my feet'; and 'don-don,' he stamped on the ground, first with one foot and then with the other to show the man. (Japanese ghosts have no feet.)

'But Urashima Taro lived three hundred years ago, that is all I know; it is written in the village chronicles,' persisted the man, who could not believe what the fisherman said.

Urashima was lost in bewilderment and trouble. He stood looking all around him, terribly puzzled, and, indeed, something in the appearance of everything was different to what he remembered before he went away, and the awful feeling came over him that what the man said was perhaps true. He seemed to be in a strange dream.

A beautiful little Purple Cloud rose out of the Box. The few days he had spent in the Sea King's palace beyond the sea had not been days at all; they had been hundreds of years, and in that time his parents had died and all the people he had ever known, and the village had written down his story. There was no use in staying here any longer. He must get back to his beautiful wife beyond the sea.

He made his way back to the beach, carrying in his hand the box which the Princess had given him. But which was the way? He could not find it alone! Suddenly he remembered the box, the Tamate-Bako.

171

Dragon; because of his youth and lack of official appointment, he was told last year to live in the Black River to nourish his nature. When he acquired a name, I would have transferred him to another post. I didn't anticipate that he would disobey my decree and offend the Great Sage.'

When Pilgrim heard these words, he smiled and said, 'How many husbands did your sister have?'

'Only one,' said Aoshun, 'and he was the Dragon King of the Jing River who was beheaded. My sister lived here as a widow and died year before last.'

'One husband and one wife,' said Pilgrim. 'How could they manage to produce so many different kinds of offspring?'

Aoshun said, 'This is what the proverb means when it says that "A dragon will produce nine species, and each species is different from the others."' Pilgrim said, 'Just now I was so vexed that I was about to use the invitation card as evidence and file suit against you at the Heavenly court, charging you with conspiracy with a fiend and kidnapping. But according to what you have told me, it's really the fault of that fellow who disobeys your instructions. I'll pardon you this time — for the sake of my relationship with you and your brothers, and on account of the fact that that dragon is young and ignorant after all. And also, you have no knowledge of that matter. Quickly dispatch someone to arrest him and rescue my master. We'll then decide what to do next.'

Aoshun at once gave this command to the prince, Moang:

'Call up immediately five hundred young soldiers of shrimps and fishes; arrest that iguana and bring him back here for indictment. Meanwhile, let us prepare some wine and a banquet as our apology to the Great Sage.'

'Dragon King,' said Pilgrim, 'you needn't be so edgy. I told you just now that I would pardon you. Why bother to prepare wine and food? I must go now with your son, for I fear that Master may be harmed and my brother is waiting for me.' Unable to detain his guest with even desperate pleadings, the old dragon asked one of his daughters to present tea. Pilgrim drank one cup of the fragrant tea while standing up and then took leave of the old dragon. He and Moang led the troops from the Western Ocean and soon arrived in the Black River. 'Worthy Prince,' said Pilgrim, 'take care to catch the fiend. I'm going ashore.'

'Have no worry, Great Sage,' said Moang. 'This little dragon will arrest him and take him up here for the Great Sage to convict him of his crime. Only after your master has been sent up also will I dare take him back to the ocean to see my father.'

Very pleased, Pilgrim left him and made the water-repellent sign with his fingers to leap out of the waves. As he reached the eastern shore, Sha Monk (who led the river god to meet him) said, 'Elder Brother, you left by the air but why did you return from the river?' Pilgrim gave a thorough account of how he slew the fish-spirit, acquired the invitation card, confronted the Dragon King, and led troops back with the dragon prince. Sha Monk was exceedingly pleased; all of them then stood on the bank to wait to receive their master, and we shall speak no more of them for the moment.

A woman riding a dragon.

175

Chapter 10

Dragons in Film and Fiction

The most popular literary dragon is arguably J.R.R. Tolkien's Smaug in *The Hobbit*; as Thorin says 'a most specially greedy, strong and wicked worm'. He appears in the film adaptations by Peter Jackson of *The Hobbit: An Unexpected Journey*; *The Hobbit: The Desolation of Smaug*; and *The Hobbit: The Battle of the Five Armies*, and is voiced by Benedict Cumberbatch. Other dragons to move from literature to the screen are in George R. R. Martin's *A Song of Ice and Fire* series televised as *Game of Thrones* and its prequel *House of the Dragon*. *Eragon*, the first book in *The Inheritance Cycle* by American fantasy writer, Christopher Paolini, was also made into a film in 2006.

Draco in the first *Dragonheart* film series is probably one of my favourites. The 1996 fantasy film has at its heart a fabulous dragon voiced by Sean Connery. And who can forget the most wonderfully named Vermithrax Pejorative in the 1981 animated film from Disney/ Paramount: *Dragonslayer*. Other typical dragons appear in the 2002 *Reign of Fire* starring Matthew McConaughey, a post-apocalyptic fantasy film set twenty years after workers inadvertently awakened dragons during a tunnel project in London and who subsequently took over the world, leaving survivalists to try to fight them.

But dragons have appeared in other guises which has added to our love of them. Take the Dragon in *Shrek* for instance or Mushu from Disney's *Mulan*. Or Falkor, the white doglike flying dragon in *The NeverEnding Story*, released in 1984 and based on the 1979 novel of the same name by Michael Ende.

Older readers might remember Elliott, Pete's Dragon from the 1977 Disney musical *Pete's Dragon* that was based on a short story called 'Pete's Dragon and the USA (Forever After)' by Seton I. Miller and S. S. Field. Disney remade the film in 2016 but it's nothing like the original.

Zog appears in a short animation released in 2018 based on the lovable character from the 2010 children's picture book by Julia Donaldson and illustrated by Axel Scheffler. The sequel, titled *Zog and the Flying Doctors* was published in 2016 and televised by BBC One for Christmas Day 2020.

The *How to Train Your Dragon* series has proved immensely popular with three films and spin-off TV series. The film is loosely based on the book by Cressida Cowell. Hiccup, the teenage Viking protagonist, wants to be a dragon slayer but after he injures the rare Night Fury dragon, he makes a prosthetic for his tail and they become, eventually, the best of friends. Of course dragons feature in many other fantasy films, from the ferocious beasts of battle to the animated cute and cuddly.

Although the last two films mentioned are primarily for children, it shows a move away from the ferocious beast of old towards a creature we could live with and love. And our own children are now being raised admiring dragons — they are no longer to be feared like the monsters under the bed.

Dragons also feature in many outstanding fiction books — some of the best are discussed below.

Robin Hobb (Margaret Astrid Lindholm Ogden) has written several books set in the realm of the Elderlings featuring dragons, but one particular series *The Rain Wild Chronicles* focuses on how man and dragon interact and live together. The dragon eggs found along the river have been affected by the acidity of the water and when they hatch the dragons are unable to fly and have lost most of their ancestral memories. The dragon keepers must take those that remain to Kelsingra, the dragons' ancient home.

There are nine books in Gordon R. Dickson's *Dragon Knight* series, the first of which was adapted into the 1982 animated movie *The Flight of Dragons* by Rankin/Bass. Jim Eckert, the Dragon Knight, ends up in a parallel medieval universe where he finds himself trapped in a dragon's body. Whilst he eventually is able to be both man and dragon, his troubles are far from over.

Naomi Novik's ten-book series, *Temeraire*, contains some great humour and of course, dragons. The novels follow Captain William Laurence and his Chinese dragon, Temeraire, and is based around events of the Napoleonic Wars. The books are packed full of intelligent fighting dragons who differ in size and type, including sea serpents.

Whilst *The Invisible Library* series by Genevieve Cogman isn't about dragons per se, dragons who can present as both human and dragon feature in the stories and is one of my favourite series that combine dragons, books and adventure!

Anne McCaffrey's *Dragonriders of Pern* is a classic dragon series running to twenty-four books. Dragons also appear in Ursula K. Le Guin's World of *Earthsea* books and Terry Pratchett's *Discworld* novels as well as Andrzej Sapkowski's *The Witcher* series. Dragons are one of the key creatures in fantasy fiction.

Edith Nesbit's 1925 short story *The Last of the Dragons* reverses your typical hero defeats dragon to rescue maiden trope. The dragon likes to be called 'Dear' and enjoys drinking petrol. He doesn't want to get involved in human affairs nor does he want to be defeated rescuing a maiden. Fortunately, the female protagonist agrees and refuses to be your typical maiden, and they work out a way for both of them to survive what would have been an ordeal. There's a surprising twist but I'll leave that for you to find out!

The Reluctant Dragon, a short story by Kenneth Grahame, is one of the loveliest depictions of a dragon. He's not aggressive and loves poetry. He becomes friends with a young boy but when St George is sent to kill him, his time is nearly up. Fortunately St George sees how friendly the dragon is and they work out a mock battle to appease the local townsfolk where the dragon is 'stabbed' but St George declares that he is reformed and no longer dangerous, so they can all live happily ever after.

So dragon fiction is as wide and varied as the myths and legends that they sprang from. And in the modern world today, dragons have also made it into the gaming world featuring in classics like Dungeons and Dragons, Spyro, World of Warcraft and Skyrim. Dragons really do be everywhere!

Epilogue

Our love of dragons isn't going to end anytime soon. More books, films and TV series for both adults and children alike will contain dragons in varying guises and in a glorious array of settings and historical periods; it seems we just can't get enough of them.

Whether dragons call to our primal instincts (see chapter one) or we just love imagining fantastical, magical beasts, they are a permanent fixture in our society and culture and have always been through time and history.

Throughout society and culture, dragons have played various roles alongside humans — as creators, enemies, treasure-hoarders, allies — the list goes on. Dragons are what we make them to be. They are part and parcel of the rich mythology and legends that are the backbone of any culture. They live in our imagination and our psyche.

We no longer have to fear them so we can love them — it's our choice — but there will always be something magical and intriguing about them. Perhaps it's because as we look to the skies we know realistically we're not going to see them but somewhere deep inside we think wouldn't it actually be quite marvellous if we did?

References

Chapter 1: Origins of the World Dragon

Sources used for chapter one include Pliny, *Naturalis Historia* (book 8); the *Anglo-Saxon Chronicle*; the *Annals of Ulster*; Chang Qu, *Chronicles of Huayang*; Carl Sagan, *The Dragons of Eden*; and JJ Cohen, *Monster Theory*.

Chapter 2: Types of Dragons

Sources for chapter two include: Pliny, *Naturalis Historia* (book eleven).
The Dragon of Wantley ballad can be found at https://allpoetry.com/
   The-Dragon-of-Wantley
Dragon folktales can vary between books and websites but you can read more about Maud and the Mordiford Dragon at https://herefordshirepast.co.uk/places/mordiford/
The Sockburn Worm: https://www.thisisdurham.com/inspire-me/durhams-unmissable-highlights/legends-of-durham/the-sockburn-worm
The Lindworm Prince: https://www.worldoftales.com/European_folktales/Norwegian_folktale_3.html#gsc.tab=0
The Lyminster Knucker: http://www.sussexarch.org.uk/saaf/dragon.html
More discussion of Ireland's wyrms can be found at http://emeraldisle.ie/the-great-wyrms-of-ireland
The Battle of Mag Mucrama can be read in full at ancienttexts.org
Marius Willem de Visser's book *The Dragon in China and Japan* has many tales of Eastern dragons.

Chapter 3: Early Myths

Main early texts like the *Rig Veda*, *Epic of Gilgamesh* and *Enuma Elish* can be found online at sacred-texts.com or in printed format.

Zoroastrian poetry can be read at https://chs.harvard.edu/chapter/7-royal-usurpations-in-iranian-literary-traditions-ii-the-evidence-of-the-sahname/

Persian dragons are discussed at https://www.iranicaonline.org/articles/azdaha-dragon-various-kinds

More about Komodo dragons can be found at https://earthstoriez.com/myth-and-legends-of-the-komodo-dragon-indonesia/

Alfred Radcliffe-Brown's article 'The Rainbow-Serpent Myth of Australia' in *The Journal of the Royal Anthropological Institute of Great Britain and Ireland* is an interesting read. As is Gerald Massey's *A Book of the Beginnings*.

You can find out more about Maori dragons at https://teara.govt.nz/en/taniwha

Chapter 4: From the Ancient World to Classical Civilisations

Theoi Greek Mythology (https://www.theoi.com/) is a wonderful website for all things Greek and dragons! They reference many primary sources including: Diodorus Siculus, *Library of History* 4. 50. 6 (trans. Oldfather); Oppian, *Halieutica* 1. 360 ff (trans. Mair); Pseudo-Apollodorus, *Bibliotheca* 2. 31-32 (trans. Aldrich); Pseudo-Apollodorus, *Bibliotheca* 3. 22 (trans. Aldrich); Pseudo-Apollodorus, *Bibliotheca* 1. 39 (trans. Aldrich); Quintus Smyrnaeus, *Fall of Troy* 12. 423 & 480 ff (trans. Way); and Orosius: book 4.

Vergil's poem *The Gnat* can be found at http://virgil.org/appendix/culex.htm

Chapter 5: Viking Dragons

Dragons feature heavily in Norse mythology including early texts like the *Prose Edda* and *Poetic Edda* but can also be found in many retellings.

You can find out more about the tricksy squirrel, Ratatoskr, at https://berloga-workshop.com/blog/247-ratatoskr.html

The Volsung Saga: *Of the Slaying of the Worm Fafnir* is quoted in Chapter XVIII but the entire text can be found at sacred-texts.com

Ragnar tales are in *The first nine books of the Danish history of Saxo Grammaticus* by Saxo, Grammaticus, d. ca.1204; Elton, Oliver, 1861-1945; Powell, F. York (Frederick York), 1850-1904.

Chapter 6: Christianity and the Dragon

Isidore of Seville wrote a chapter on snakes and dragons in chapter IV of Book XII of his *Etymologiae*. Other works cited are Hugh of Fouilloy's *De avibus* and the Bible.

Caxton's *Golden Legend* can be found at https://sourcebooks.fordham.edu/basis/goldenlegend/gl-vol3-george.asp

More about the Order of the Dragon is at http://www.holyromanempireassociation.com/order-of-the-dragon-Ordo-Draconum.html

Chapter 7: The Medieval Dragon in Folklore and Literature

The full poem Beowulf can be found at https://www.poetryfoundation.org/poems/50114/beowulf-modern-english-translation

More about Bevis of Hampton is available at https://d.lib.rochester.edu/crusades/text/bevis-of-hampton#:~:text=Bevis%20of%20Hampton%20(c.,contains%20the%20earliest%20extant%20version

Guy of Warwick's story can be found in Merridew (1821), *The Noble and Renowned History of Guy, Earl of Warwick: Containing a Full and True Account of His Many Famous and Valiant Actions, Remarkable and Brave Exploits, and Noble and Renowned Victories.*

The stories of King Arthur, Merlin and Welsh dragons can be found in many books including *Historia Brittonum* (History of the Britons) and Malory's *Morte d'Arthur.*

The travels of Sir John Mandeville can be found at https://www.gutenberg.org/files/782/782-h/782-h.htm

Chapter 8: Dragon Tales from the West

Sources are given throughout but Edmund Spenser's *The Fairie Queen* can be found at https://www.gutenberg.org/files/15272/15272-h/15272-h.htm#canto_I

Chapter 9: Dragon Tales from the East

Sources are given throughout the chapter.

Chapter 10: Dragons in Film and Fiction

All films and books are available at your favourite retailers or streaming services!

Illustration Credits

All integrated images are Wikimedia Commons, public domain, except:

Page 7   Public domain image: https://www.flickr.com/photos/ internetarchivebookimages/14753363275/

Page 36   Persian Miniature Paintings (Wellcome Collection, Attribution 4.0 International — CC BY 4.0.)

Page 39   Public domain image: https://www.flickr.com/photos/ internetarchivebookimages/14801742983/

Page 43   Batara f.s simangunsong (Wikimedia Commons, Attribution 4.0 International — CC BY 4.0.)

Page 64   Ziko van Dijk (Wikimedia Commons, Attribution 4.0 International — CC BY 4.0.)

Page 176 A Chinese woman with flowers in her hand rides a dragon (Colour woodcut by a Chinese artist. Wellcome Collection. Public Domain Mark.)

Further Reading

Non-fiction

Allen, Judy & Griffiths, Jeanne, *The Book of the Dragon*.
Bruce, Scott G. (ed.), *The Penguin Book of Dragons*.
Hargreaves, Joyce, *A Little History of Dragons*.
Honegger, Thomas, *Introducing the Medieval Dragon*.
Jones, David, *An Instinct for Dragons*.
Ogden, Daniel, *Dragons, Serpents, and Slayers in the Classical and Early Christian Worlds: A Sourcebook*.
Ogden, Daniel, *The Dragon in the West*.
Sagan, Carl, *The Dragons of Eden*.
Shuker, Karl, *Dragons: A Natural History*.
Simpson, Jacqueline, *British Dragons*.
Steer, Dugald, *Dragonology: The Complete Book of Dragons (Ology Series)*.

Fiction

Brennan, Marie, *A Natural History of Dragons*.
Ende, Michael, *The Neverending Story*.
Hobb, Robin, *The Dragon Keeper*.
Lackey, Mercedes, *Joust*.
McCaffrey, Anne, *Dragonflight*.
Novik, Naomi, *His Majesty's Dragon*.
Owen, James A., *Here, There Be Dragons*.
Paolini, Christopher, *Eragon*.
Pratchett, Terry, *Guards! Guards!*

Preiss, Brian and Reaves, Michael, *Dragonworld.*
Rawn, Melanie, *Dragon Prince.*
Roberts, Nora, *The Awakening.*
Shannon, Samantha, *The Priory of the Orange Tree.*
Stasheff, Christopher, *Her Majesty's Wizard.*
Tolkien, J.R.R., *The Hobbit, or There and Back Again.*
Walton, Jo, *Tooth and Claw.*
Zahn, Timothy, *Dragon and Thief.*